PRESS and MEDIA ACCESS to the CRIMINAL COURTROOM

Recent Titles from Quorum Books

The Modern Economics of Housing: A Guide to Theory and Policy for Finance and Real Estate Professionals
Randall Johnston Pozdena

Productivity and Quality through Science and Technology
Y. K. Shetty and Vernon M. Buehler, editors

Interactive Corporate Compliance: An Alternative to Regulatory Compulsion
Jay A. Sigler and Joseph Murphy

Voluntary Corporate Liquidations
Ronald J. Kudla

Business-Government Relations and Interdependence: A Managerial and Analytic Perspective
John M. Stevens, Steven L. Wartick, and John W. Bagby

Career Growth and Human Resource Strategies: The Role of the Human Resource Professional in Employee Development
Manuel London and Edward M. Mone, editors

Guide to International Real Estate Investment
M. A. Hines

Occupational Job Evaluation: A Research-Based Approach to Job Classification
Wilfredo R. Manese

The Professionals' Guide to Fund Raising, Corporate Giving, and Philanthropy: People Give to People
Lynda Lee Adams-Chau

Financial Forecasting and Planning: A Guide for Accounting, Marketing, and Planning Managers
Sharon Hatten Garrison, Wallace N. Davidson, Jr., and Michael A. Garrison

Professional Accounting Practice Management
Joseph T. Kastantin

The New Oil Crisis and Fuel Economy Technologies: Preparing the Light Transportation Industry for the 1990's
Deborah Lynn Bleviss

PRESS and MEDIA ACCESS to the CRIMINAL COURTROOM

WARREN FREEDMAN

Q QUORUM BOOKS

New York · Westport, Connecticut · London

Library of Congress Cataloging-in-Publication Data

Freedman, Warren.
Press and media access to the criminal courtroom / Warren Freedman.
p. cm.
Bibliography: p.
Includes index.
ISBN 0-89930-328-5 (lib. bdg. : alk. paper)
1. Conduct of court proceedings—United States. 2. Video tapes in courtroom proceedings—United States. 3. Criminal courts—United States. 4. Free press and fair trial—United States. I. Title.
KF8725.F74 1988
345.73'075—dc19
[347.30575] 88-4039

British Library Cataloguing in Publication Data is available.

Library of Congress Catalog Card Number: 88-4039
ISBN: 0-89930-328-5

First published in 1988 by Quorum Books

Greenwood Press, Inc.
88 Post Road West, Westport, Connecticut 06881

Printed in the United States of America

The paper used in this book complies with the Permanent Paper Standard issued by the National Information Standards Organization (Z39.48-1984).

10 9 8 7 6 5 4 3 2 1

Families have been the vehicle for success over the centuries, and their cooperation and understanding are responsible for this writing: my loving wife Esther Freedman, a psychiatric social worker; my son Dr. Douglas Freedman, an orthodontist; my daughter Debbie Stiebel, mother of three grandchildren and elementary school teacher in Avon, Connecticut; and my youngest daughter, Miriam, a successful art director in a well-known New York City advertising agency.

Contents

Preface ix

1. The First Amendment and the Public's Right of Access 1

2. The First Amendment and Freedom of Press 11

3. The Sixth Amendment and the Fair Trial Guarantee 23

4. Closure of the Criminal Courtroom 31

5. Photographing, Broadcasting, and Televising in the Criminal Courtroom 41
   Appendix 61

6. The Right to Gather Information versus the Right to Disseminate Information 69

7. Courtroom Cameras, Electronic Media Equipment, and the Trial Lawyer 79

8. Prejudicial Trial Publicity and the Conduct of the Trial Lawyer 87

9. Civil Trials and the Right of Access for Press and Media 105

10. Public and Press and Media Access to the Courtroom in England 115

Bibliography 121

Index to Cases 123

Subject Index 127

Preface

A quarter century ago I authored an important article titled "News Media Coverage of Criminal Cases and the Right to a Fair Trial," which appeared in volume 40 of the Nebraska Law Review (1961). The title is somewhat anachronistic because in today's economy the press and media are not necessarily concerned with "news" but with "entertainment." The accused's right to a speedy and fair criminal trial, for example, is therefore less of a shibboleth of the press and media today; it is only incidental to the "entertainment" that is being sold under the guise of presenting the "news" to the American public. Whether the changing concept of press and media merits the same protection as is generally afforded the "news" is an open question. Yet the unanswered question persists, unless we create a new concept of "news-entertainment" which is more consonant with reality.

Nevertheless, it is important that the accused's rights to a speedy and fair trial be guaranteed; and the press and media are indeed the bulwarks against those forces that would preclude such guarantees. The speedy trial usually means a fair trial, and a fair trial presumes a speedy trial. Giving the press and media access to the criminal courtroom, whether for news or for entertainment or for both—means that someone may be sufficiently concerned about protecting these basic constitutional rights alongside the protection afforded the press and media under the First Amendment.

Barring radio, television, and newspaper coverages from the criminal courtroom is primarily rationalized on the grounds of maintaining the dignity and decorum of the courtroom, which is then more conducive to protecting the constitutional rights of the criminal defendant to a speedy and fair trial. But these modern-day electronic coverages, including still photography, do not interfere with the conduct of the criminal trial, especially where the trial judge has the instrument of control and supervision, and when the press and media abide by their own codes of conduct. A criminal courtroom need not be forced open all the time if the press and media have rights of access that are respected by the judiciary. In short, press and media should make application for permission to broadcast, televise, report, or photograph the criminal proceedings. There should be little or no restraint whether the proceedings are pre-trial (like evidence suppression hearings) or even post-trial (like appeal motions). Good faith is necessary on both sides of the curtain, and only then is the public's right to know (or to be entertained) assured.

PRESS and MEDIA ACCESS to the CRIMINAL COURTROOM

1

The First Amendment and the Public's Right of Access

The First Amendment to the U.S. Constitution provides that "Congress shall make no law . . . abridging the freedom of speech or of the press." These noble words have served as the basis for recognition of the axiom that both the public and the press and media have a fundamental right of access to courtroom proceedings and a right to attend criminal trials.[1] The public's right of access is grounded on the Anglo-American tradition of open criminal proceedings and the need for public scrutiny of the judicial process.[2] However, this historical basis for open criminal proceedings is subject to the Sixth Amendment's protection of the criminal defendant's right to receive a fair trial.[3] A defendant apparently has no right to a secret or closed criminal trial, as more particularly manifest in state court proceedings like Phoenix Newspapers Incorporated v. Jennings,[4] where the Arizona Supreme Court emphasized that the criminal defendant was not entitled to have the public (and the press) excluded from a preliminary criminal hearing despite the claim that harmful and prejudicial publicity would endanger the defendant's right to a fair trial by an impartial jury.

On the other hand, the New York decision of United Press Association v. Valente[5] held that the First Amendment right of access to the criminal courtroom was not abridged by an exclusionary order of the New York court denying to the public opportunity to see and hear what transpired at trial. A criminal defendant, however, cannot waive the right of the public to have a trial open to the public view because a crime is a public wrong in which the community is deeply interested, and therefore the public has a right to observe the administration of criminal justice.[6] The Oregon Supreme Court in State ex rel Oregonian Publishing Co. v. Deiz[7] apparently ruled that the public could be excluded from the juvenile criminal courtroom when the juvenile court was of the opinion that privacy would promote the goal of juvenile justice; here a thirteen-year-old girl was in custody in connection with the drowning of a younger child.[8] Yet the highest Oregon court could not overcome the express language of the Oregon Constitution[9] that "no court shall be secret, but justice shall be administered . . . openly," and so the trial court order barring the public and the press was declared to be invalid, subject, however, to the trial court's discretion "to control access by members of the press or public who would overcrowd the courtroom, attempt to interfere in the proceedings, or otherwise obstruct the proceedings." The dissenting opinion of Justice Howell cited numerous examples such as bastardy-filiation proceedings, guardianship proceedings, and rape trials where "in the interests of justice, the legislature had determined that the press and the public may or should be excluded," without violating the Oregon Constitution.

The English common law rule of open proceedings was embodied in colonial charters and state constitutions. The New Jersey Constitution of 1676, for example, provided for the right of the public to attend trials.[10] Later, the language was shortened to command that "all courts shall be open," coupled with the mandate that every person shall obtain remedy by due course of law, or that justice shall be impartially administered, or both.[11] The thrust soon took the form of an independent right on the part of the public to attend civil and criminal trials and not simply a right in favor of the litigants to demand a public proceeding.[12] The Ohio court in E. W. Scripps Co. v. Fulton[13] observed in 1955:

> It can never be claimed that in a democratic society the public has no interest in or does not have the right to observe the administration of justice. The open courtroom is as necessary and important in the interest of supporting the administration of justice as is the protection of the rights of a member of the public when on trial for a criminal offense. . . . The defendents cannot waive the right of the people to insist that the proceedings of the courts, insofar as

practicable and in the interest of the public health and public morals, be open to public view. . . . [14]

The U.S. Supreme Court in its 1986 opinion in Press-Enterprise Co. v. Superior Court of California[15] opined that "the right to an open public (criminal) trial is a shared right of the accused and the public, the common concern being the assurance of fairness . . . the explicit Sixth Amendment right of the accused is no less protective of a public trial than the implicit First Amendment right of the press and the public."[16] Chief Justice Warren Burger, citing the earlier 1984 case of Press-Enterprise Co. v. Superior Court,[17] observed that "since the development of trial by jury, the process of selection of jurors has presumptively been a public process." In Richmond Newspapers Inc. v. Virginia,[18] the Court reviewed the early history of England's open trials from the day when a trial was much like a town meeting. In the days before the Norman Conquest, criminal cases were brought before "moots," a collection of freemen in the community. Indeed,

the public trial, one of the essential qualities of a court of justice in England, was recognized early in the colonies. There were risks, of course, inherent in such a "town meeting" trial. . . . The modern trial with jurors open to interrogation for possible bias is a far cry from the "town meeting trial" of ancient English practice. Yet even our modern procedural protections have their origin in the ancient common law principle, which provided, not for closed proceedings, but rather for rules of conduct for those who attend trials. . . . Openness in criminal trials, including the selection of jurors, "enhances both the basic fairness of the criminal trial and the appearance of fairness so essential to public confidence in the system."[19]

But the Court warned that "there are some limited circumstances" in which the rights of the criminal accused might override the qualified First Amendment right of access.[20]

The public right of access to criminal trial proceedings is not limited to the courtroom but also encompasses preliminary hearings. Indeed, the vast majority of states have concluded that the same tradition of accessibility that applies to criminal trials applies to preliminary hearings.[21] In Press-Enterprise Co. v. Superior Court of California,[22] the U.S. Supreme Court also concluded that the right of access applies to preliminary hearings as conducted in California. Preliminary hearings ''conducted before neutral and detached magistrates'' have long been ''open to the public'':

> In the celebrated trial of Aaron Burr for treason, for example, with Chief Justice Marshall sitting as trial judge, the probable cause hearing was held in the Hall of the House of Delegates of Virginia, the courtroom being too small to accommodate the crush of interested citizens. . . . From Burr until the present day, the near uniform practice of State and federal courts has been to conduct preliminary hearings in open court. . . . Indeed, public access to criminal trials and the selection of jurors is essential to the proper functioning of the criminal justice system.[23]

The accused has the right to appear personally at the preliminary hearing, to be represented by counsel, to cross-examine hostile witnesses, to present exculpatory evidence, and to exclude illegally obtained evidence against him or her. If the magistrate or hearing officer determines that probable cause exists, the accused is bound over for trial. Denial of the transcripts of a preliminary hearing would frustrate the ''community therapeutic value'' of openness of criminal trials, according to the highest Court, which also cited in its 1984 opinion Reik's ''The Compulsion to Confess'':

> The value of openness lies in the fact that people not actually attending trials can have confidence that standards of fairness are being observed; the sure knowledge that anyone is free to attend gives assurance that established procedures are being followed and deviations will become known. Openness thus enhances both the basic fairness of the criminal trial and the appearance of fairness so essential to public confidence in the system.[24]

Indeed, ''Preliminary hearings shall be closed only if specific findings are made demonstrating that, first, there is substantial probability that the defendant's right to a fair trial will be prejudiced by publicity that closure would prevent, and second, reasonable alternatives to closure cannot adequately protect the defendant's free trial rights.'' The dissenting opinion of Justice John Paul Stevens held that

> it is incontrovertible that a common law right of access did not inhere in preliminary proceedings at the time the First Amendment was adopted, and that the Framers and ratifiers of that provision could not have intended such proceedings to remain open. . . . The presence of a legitimate reason for

closure in this case requires an affirmance. The constitutionally-grounded fair trial interests of the accused if he is bound over for trial, and the reputational interests of the accused if he is not, provide a substantial reason for delaying access to the transcript for at least the short time before trial.

The First U.S. Court of Appeals in In re Globe Newspaper Co.[25] considered whether the public has a First Amendment right of access to pre-trial bail proceedings, after first observing that the historical basis for open criminal trials did not extend to pre-trial proceedings. But the federal appellate court in 1984 focused on the policy concerns that supported public access, and the court concluded that the need for public scrutiny of trial proceedings, as well as the importance of the public's understanding of the trial process, mandated access to both trial and pre-trial proceedings. The court reasoned that the problem of access was aggravated by the accused's challenge to the admissibility of evidence obtained through electronic surveillance.[26] If the evidence was admissible at trial, the public's access to the wiretap information would be seriously delayed; or if the evidence was inadmissible at trial, closure of the pre-trial bail hearing would be a crucial measure in protecting the defendant's fair trial by excluding it from potential jurors.

Courts must meet three procedural requisites before closing a pre-trial proceeding: the public and the press must have an opportunity to voice objections to closure; the court must weigh the competing interests involved and consider alternatives to closure; and the court must draw any closure order as restrictively as possible so as to preserve the concept of open trial and open pre-trial in criminal proceedings. The public's right to scrutinize and freely discuss criminal trials applies equally well to pre-trial bail hearings. Release on bail may prevent trial if the defendant flees the jurisdiction, and a denial of bail may raise profound interests as to personal liberty.

Still another important issue surrounding the public access to criminal proceedings revolves about access to information controlled by the government. In Houchins v. KQED, Inc.,[27] the U.S. Supreme Court directly confronted the issue when the communications media sought access to inspect a prison where a prisoner had committed suicide after a judicial finding that the prison conditions were "shocking and debasing." All seven participating justices agreed that the press had no constitutional right of access to the government's information superior to that of the public and that the court has limited institutional capacity to enforce a right of access to information in the government's hands.[28] The right to inspect and copy judicial records, however, is an ancient doctrine stemming from an act of Parliament in the year 1372. As long as the person has a proprietary interest in a judicial document or needs a judicial document as evidence to enforce a right of access in court, he or she is entitled to access.[29] In the United States all citizens have the right of access to judicial records because all citizens should be free to view their government in operation.[30] As Justice Oliver Wendell Holmes expressed it, "It is desirable that the trial . . . should take place under the public eye, not because the controversies of one citizen with another are of public concern, but because it is of the highest moment that those who administer justice should always act under the sense of public responsibility, and that every citizen should be able to satisfy himself with his own eyes as to the mode in which a public duty is performed."[31]

There are, however, limitations on this right of access to criminal court records, as noted by the U.S. Supreme Court in 1978 in Nixon v. Warner Communications.[32] Here the Court would not allow the use of judicial records to satisfy "private spite or to promote public scandal"[33] or as a "source of business information that might harm a litigant's competitive standing."[34] Indeed, it would appear that it is within the sound discretion of the trial judge to allow or disallow access to judicial records. However, several U.S. circuit courts of appeals have recently upheld claims of a common law right to inspect and copy evidentiary material in criminal trials,[35] and several other federal appellate courts have denied such access, especially to the media, to inspect and copy audiotapes that the prosecution had used in a criminal trial.[36] Yet the impact of the U.S. Supreme Court's 1980 decision in Richmond Newspapers, Inc. v. Virginia,[37] holding that the public and the press have a First Amendment right to attend criminal trials, has not resolved the conflict of views.

Two years later, Globe Newspaper Co. v. Superior Court,[38] further defined the First Amendment right of access to attend criminal trials but concluded that the right was not absolute; the qualified right of access may be overcome if a closure order is "necessitated by a compelling governmental interest, and is narrowly tailored to serve that interest."[39] Here the Massachusetts statute that promoted closure in order to protect young rape victims from further trauma and embarrassment was held unconstitutional.[40] In 1983 in Associated Press v. District Court,[41] the Ninth U.S. Court of Appeals held that the First Amendment required that a court provide access to pre-trial documents filed in a highly publicized narcotics trial of a public figure. The trial judge, by filing a document under seal, had impermissibly undermined the First Amendment presumption of access to criminal proceedings. The Second U.S. Court of Appeals in 1987 in United States v. Biaggi[42] ruled, however, that a qualified First Amendment right to documents sealed at a pre-trial criminal hearing may exist but that it must be balanced against the individual's right of privacy and the individual's fair trial rights, as well as the rights of innocent third parties. The federal wiretap law cannot override the constitutional rights that may be harmed by the disclosure.

The Third U.S. Court of Appeals on August 14, 1987, in United States v. Raffoul, gave both the public and the press-media the right to have a hearing before a courtroom closure. Here the defendant, charged with importing heroin into the United States, was testifying about alleged threats to his family when the trial judge ordered the courtroom closed, and representatives of the press and public who were present at the criminal trial up to that point were ejected. One news reporter filed a motion to intervene and for access to the sealed transcript, and the federal appellate court agreed that the petition entitled both the press and the public to a full hearing within a reasonable time in advance of closure. Earlier in 1987 the New York Court of Appeals in Associated Press v. Bell[43] had unanimously agreed that the First Amendment protects an affirmative right of access by the public and by the press-media to criminal hearings, including pre-trial suppression hearings.

NOTES

1. See generally 39 Vand L Rev 1465 (1986).

2. See generally 29 Suffolk U L Rev 129 (1985).

3. See, for example, Estes v. Texas, 381 US 532 (1965), where the U.S. Supreme Court overturned the defendant's conviction due to extensive publicity occasioned by videotaping, and Rideau v. Louisiana, 373 US 723 (1963), where a robbery-murder conviction was reversed due to a local telecast of defendant's confession.

4. 107 Ariz 557, 490 P2d 563 (1971).

5. 308 NY 71, 123 NE2d 777 (1954).

6. See E. W. Scripps Co. v. Fulton, 100 Ohio App 157, 125 NE2d 896 (1955).

7. 289 Ore 277, 613 P2d 23 (1980).

8. The Oregon statute (ORS 419.498(1)) provided that "unless the child or parents otherwise request, the general public shall be excluded and only such persons admitted as the judge finds have a proper interest in the case or the work of the court. The judge may exclude the public during any portion of the hearing in which it appears that the presence of the public may embarrass a witness or party or otherwise prejudice the reception of trustworthy evidence." Chief Justice Denecke opined that the statute "grants broad authority to the juvenile court judge to control access to the courtroom. . . . We conclude that the press are members of the public and may be excluded when the juvenile court is of the opinion that privacy would promote the goals of juvenile justice."

9. Article I, sec. 10 thereof.

10. Charter XXIII of the Charter or Fundamental Laws of West New Jersey, 5 Thorpe, American Charters, Constitutions and Organic Laws, 1492-1908 (1909).

11. See State ex rel Herald Mail Co. v. Hamilton, 267 SE2d 544 (W.Va., 1980) at p. 549.

12. See, for example, Cohen v. Everett City Council, 85 Wash2d 385, 535 P2d 801 (1975).

13. Infra note 6.

14. At pp. 162, 167, 900.

15. 106 S Ct 2735 (1986).

16. Citing Waller v. Georgia, 467 US 39 (1984).

17. 464 US 501 (1984).

18. 448 US 555 (1980).

19. Infra note 15.

20. Id.

21. See Arkansas Television Co. v. Tedder, 281 Ark 152, 662 SW2d 174 (1983); Miami Herald Publishing Co. v. Lewis, 426 So2d 1 (Fla., 1982); R. W. Page Corp. v. Lumpkin, 249 Ga 576, 292 SE2d 815 (1982); and State v. Williams, 93 NJ 39, 459 A2d 641 (1983).

22. Infra note 15.

23. Infra note 15.

24. Infra note 17 at pp. 508, 823.

25. 729 F2d 47 (1st Cir., 1984).

26. See 18 USC 2518(10)(a) on the right to move for suppression of wire or oral communication at trial on the ground that the interception was unlawful. Also infra note 2 at p. 134.

27. 98 S Ct 2588 (1978).

28. See Tribe, American Constitutional Law (1978) at pp. 68–69.

29. Infra note 1 at p. 1467; note 16 Ga L Rev 659 (1982).

30. See Nixon v. Warner Communications, Inc., 435 US 589 (1978).

31. See Crowley v. Pulsifer, 137 Mass 392 (1884).

32. Infra note 30.

33. Id.

34. Infra note 30 at p. 598.

35. See United States v. Myers, 635 F2d 945 (2d Cir., 1980); United States v. Jenrette, 653 F2d 609 (D.C. Cir., 1981); and United States v. Criden, 648 F2d 814 (3d Cir., 1981).

36. See Belo Broadcasting Corp. v. Clark, 654 F2d 423 (5th Cir., 1981).

37. 448 US 555 (1980).

38. 457 US 596 (1982).

39. Id at pp. 606–7.

40. Infra note 1 at p. 1477.

41. 705 F2d 1143 (9th Cir., 1983).

42. ———F2d——— (2d Cir., Sept. 28, 1987).

43. ———NY2d———, ———NE2d——— (June 9, 1987).

2

The First Amendment and Freedom of Press

The First Amendment of the U.S. Constitution ensures that "Congress shall make no law . . . abridging the freedom of speech, or of the press." These stark terms ensure the free flow of information essential to the functioning of a democratic society.[1] This First Amendment language also promotes an informed discussion of governmental affairs, including those conducted in courts—hence the right of access of the press and media to the criminal courtroom.

Justification for open trials accessible to the press and media harks back to the traditional Anglo-Saxon distrust of secret trials ascribed to the Star Chamber. In those early days, the English town, village, or shire, rather than the national government, had responsibility for apprehending criminals, and it was therefore natural to expect members of the public to report the facts of the crime and then for other members of the public to judge the guilt of the offender. From these humble beginnings grew the modern jury system. Today access to criminal proceedings by the public and by the press and media constitutes a safeguard against any attempt to use the court as an instrument of persecution; notice to witnesses who will be encouraged to give voluntarily pertinent and truthful evidence; and a public feeling of confidence in judicial remedies by observing the court in action.[2] The famous Blackstone in 1768 opined that

> this open examination of witnesses viva voce, in the presence of all mankind, is much more conducive to the clearing up of truth, than private and secret

examination taken down in writing before an officer or his clerk, "as was the usual practice" in the ecclesiastical courts, and all others that have borrowed their practices from the civil law; for a witness may frequently depose that in private which he will be ashamed to testify in a public and solemn tribunal. There, "too" an artful or careless scribe may make a witness speak what he never meant by dressing up his depositions in his own forms and language; but he is here at liberty to correct and explain his meaning, if misunderstood, which he can never do after a written deposition is once taken.[3]

The role of the press and media is to report what transpired within the criminal proceeding, for the press and the media not only constitute part of the general public (and are therefore entitled to the enjoyment of the public's right of access to criminal proceedings)[4] but are also entitled to the First Amendment rights of free speech and of the press in their special capacity as an entity gathering and disseminating information. The special status of the press and media rests on "the realistic recognition that it is impossible for any meaningful number of the general public to abandon their daily pursuits to attend trials, and a further acknowledgement that the press has valuable expertise in ferreting out information difficult for the general public to obtain."[5] The U.S. Supreme Court aptly expressed this "surrogate relationship" of the press and media to the general public in Cox Broadcasting Corp. v. Cohn:[6]

In a society in which each individual has but limited time and resources with which to observe at first hand the operation of his government, he relies necessarily upon the press (and media) to bring to him in convenient form the facts of these operations. Great responsibility is accordingly placed upon the news media to report fully and accurately the proceedings of government, and official records and documents open to the public are the basic data of governmental operations. Without the information provided by the press (and media) most of us and many of our representatives would be unable to vote intelligently or to register opinions on the administration of government generally. With respect to judicial proceedings in particular, the function of the press serves to guarantee the fairness of trials and to bring to bear the beneficial effects of public scrutiny upon the administration of justice.[7]

Indeed, a robust, unfettered, and creative press and media is "indispensable to government by free discussion and to the intelligent operation of a democratic society."[8]

Depriving the press and media of access to the criminal courtroom, despite the clear language of the First Amendment, has been delineated in terms of "prior restraint." In 1931 in Near v. Minnesota,[9] the U.S. Supreme Court formulated its antagonism to any prior restraint; here the Court held unconstitutional a Minnesota statute authorizing issuance of an injunction against publishing malicious and scandalous publications. The impermissibility of prior restraint of the press and media is today the cornerstone of First Amendment protection afforded to the press and media. Forty years later, in Organization for a Better Austin v. Keefe,[10] the Court emphasized that there is a strong presumption against the constitutional validity of any prior restraint. The same year, in New York Times Co. v. United States,[11] the Court found that the government had not proved that national security justified restraining the newspaper from publishing the Pentagon Papers. Indeed a prior restraint on speech and publication constitutes an impermissible restraint on First Amendment rights. And the 1976 decision of Nebraska Press Association v. Stuart[12] overturned a court order prohibiting the press from reporting the details of a crime and its investigation. Both the prosecutor and the defense counsel had requested a restraint on the media because of the reasonable likelihood that prejudicial news coverage would make it impossible to impanel an impartial jury. The U.S. Supreme Court unanimously struck down the court order and fashioned a three-part test designed to foreclose prior restraints in all but the most compelling circumstances. Before a prior restraint can issue, the trial court must determine that (1) the nature and extent of pre-trial publicity would be so intense and pervasive that it would impinge on the defendant's right to a fair trial; (2) other preventive devices would be unlikely to protect adequately the fairness of the trial; and (3) the order would prevent the threatened danger from infringing upon the defendant's fair trial right.

If the three-part test is not satisfied, then the prior restraint of the press and media is unjustified and unconstitutional, as it was in Des Moines Register & Tribune Co. v. Osmundson,[13] where the trial judge tried to enjoin disclosure of the identity of the jurors in the criminal trial. In the Nebraska Press decision, the highest Court agreed that the publicity could undermine the defendant's right to a fair trial: but since the trial judge had not considered other alternatives and because the evidence in the record did not support a finding that possible alternatives would have been ineffective, the Nebraska court order was struck down.[14]

Closure motions are designed to keep out the public and the press and media generally in the interest of protecting the defendant. The Ninth U.S. Court of Appeals in 1982 in United States v. Brooklier[15] adopted a strict standard for closing pre-trial criminal proceedings: "Those excluded from the proceeding must be afforded a reasonable opportunity to state their objections, and the reasons supporting closure must be articulated in findings."[16] Interestingly the court here favored the test advocated by the dissenting opinion of Justice Harry Blackmun in Gannett Co. v. DePasquale.[17] The accused seeking closure of the criminal courtroom to the public and the press and media must establish that

> it is strictly and inescapably necessary in order to protect the fair-trial guarantee [because] a substantial probability [exists] that irreparable damage to his fair trial right will result from conducting the proceeding in public, a substantial probability [exists] that alternatives to closure will not protect adequately his right to a fair trial, and a substantial probability [exists] that closure will be effective in protecting against the perceived harm.[18]

How to measure the nature and extent of the harm to a defendant's right to a fair trial is simply not determinable!

Gag orders are a phenomenon that occur frequently in criminal proceedings, as illustrated by KPNX v. Superior Court.[19] Here a television station reporter and a courtroom sketch artist were covering a criminal trial when the trial judge issued an order mandating that the sketches of jurors be shown to him before being televised. (A rule of the Arizona Supreme Court prohibited television camera coverage of jurors.) The Arizona Supreme Court, however, considered the order to be an unlawful prior restraint of expression; but the court refused to hold that a media liaison order that limited contact by the media with persons involved in the criminal trial was an unlawful gag order, for the order did not abridge the media's right to attend and report on the criminal trial. Indeed, the U.S. Supreme Court in Sheppard v. Maxwell[20] in 1966 had recognized the court's power to curtail statements by attorneys, witnesses, jurors, and even court personnel, especially where there is a "reasonable likelihood that prejudicial news . . . will prevent a fair trial."[21] Yet the Sixth U.S. Court of Appeals in CBS Inc. v. Young[22] has held that a gag order directed solely at trial participants constituted an unlawful prior restraint on the press and media. The Eleventh U.S. Court of Appeals in United States v.

Hastings[23] ruled that the press's right of access to observe criminal trials did not extend to televising, recording, or broadcasting criminal trials. The right of the press and media of access to criminal courtrooms is not absolute:

> Just as a government may impose reasonable time, place, and manner restrictions upon the use of its streets in the interest of such objectives as the free flow of traffic . . . so may a trial judge, in the interest of the fair administration of justice, impose reasonable limitations on access to a trial. "The question in a particular case is whether that control is exerted so as not to deny or unwarrantedly abridge . . . the opportunities for the communication of thought and the discussion of public questions immemorially associated with resort to public places."[24]

The Fifth U.S. Court of Appeals in In re Express-News Corp.[25] expressed the caveat: "A court cannot . . . restrict the journalistic right to gather news unless it is narrowly tailored to prevent a substantial threat to the administration of justice."[26] Still, judges can place limitations on public statements made by lawyers, litigants, and court officials for good cause in order to ensure a fair trial.[27]

Occasionally a criminal conviction has been reversed on the ground that the publicity surrounding the trial was prejudicial enough to deny the defendant's right to a fair trial. In Rideau v. Louisiana,[28] the U.S. Supreme Court found that the defendant's confession had been filmed and then televised on three occasions before the criminal trial for murder began. In Sheppard v. Maxwell,[29] the highest Court found pervasive and opinionated publicity prior to as well as during the murder trial. And in Irvin v. Dowd,[30] publicity was so widespread and prejudicial that newspapers referred to the accused as "confessed slayer of six." Indeed local newspapers featured citizen opinions not only on the accused's guilt but about the punishment the accused should receive. On the other hand, in Murphy v. Florida,[31] despite the jurors' knowledge of the defendant's prior convictions for murder and robbery, the highest Court affirmed the conviction for robbery, pointing out that there was no evidence of actual prejudice in the voir dire.

While the First Amendment is clear as to the right of the public and of the press and media to attend criminal trials, it is interesting to note that several states have held that their state constitutions pose no obstacle to statutes or rules directing or permitting the closure of "preliminary'' criminal proceedings.[32] California and Nevada decisions, for example, have held that their constitutions conferred no public right of access that prevented a magistrate from exercising statutory discretion to close a preliminary criminal hearing.[33] The preliminary criminal hearing, while varying in content from state to state, serves as a sounding board for the prosecution to introduce sufficient evidence of probable cause that the accused committed the particular crime. As delineated in State of Utah v. Anderson,[34] ''The fundamental purpose served by the preliminary examination is the ferreting out of groundless and improvident prosecutions. The effectuation of this primary purpose relieves the accused from the substantial degradation and expense incident to a modern criminal trial when the charges against him are unwarranted or the evidence insufficient.''[35] The preliminary criminal hearing represents a critical stage in the criminal process and a vital part of the criminal prosecution. Indeed the public and the press and media have a constitutional right of access, although the press and media must exercise that right of access with responsibility for their ''high public trust.''[36] This public trust cannot be used as a shield to favor journalists and television reporters, for example, who must still comply with ordinary legal obligations imposed on the general body of citizens, although it is argued that this lack of special considerations for the press and media might impair the ability of the press and media to gather and publish the news. The U.S. Supreme Court in Branzburg v. Nixon[37] brushed aside the plea of a journalist not to be forced to reveal in grand jury proceedings the source of his information, the disclosure of which would allegedly be ''to the detriment of the free flow of information protected by the First Amendment.''[38] The highest Court put the needs of the administration of justice first and refused to recognize the ''shield privilege.''

The press achieved recognition of its favored position from the New Mexico Supreme Court in State ex rel New Mexico Press Association v. Kaufman.[39] The court recognized the procedural and substantive rights of the press and media against requests to restrict news coverage of criminal cases. Here the murder trial of the first of thirty-eight penitentiary inmates accused of murder prompted the defendant trial judge to enter orders prohibiting any photographs of the accused within the courtroom areas, barring publication of the names of prospective or selected jurors, and requiring reporters covering the trial to ''preserve articles, tapes, or transcripts, if such are made, until ten days after the verdict. The highest state court reversed the trial judge on all three restraints, pointing out that the issue of allowing cameras in the courtroom was not of constitutional dimension, for it had been expressly authorized by the court's own Code of Judicial Conduct.[40] The trial court did not have the authority to impose orders on nonparticipants in the trial who had First Amendment rights, and the ban on publication of jurors' names constituted an unlawful prior restraint. The New Mexico Supreme Court mandated notice and an opportunity to be heard before restraints are imposed on the press and media. The hearing must occur prior to the criminal trial, if possible, but short notice, proof of affidavit, and abbreviated informal hearings are acceptable. The trial court in New Mexico must consider all reasonable alternatives, determine if the restriction sought is the least restrictive means available, and determine if the restriction could in fact be effective. In addition, no court order can be broader in application or duration than necessary to accomplish its purpose. Also, the trial court must make oral or written findings to support any restrictive order on the press and media.

A similar stance was taken by the Washington Supreme Court in Seattle Times Co. v. Ishikawa[41] with respect to pre-trial criminal hearings and the transcripts or records of such preliminary criminal proceedings. On May 12, 1987, in In the Matter of the Application to a Judge by the Providence Journal Company and Its Executive Editor Charles M. Hauser in Criminal Contempt,[42] the First U.S. Court of Appeals castigated the press for ignoring a restraining order of the federal district court in Rhode Island. The trial court had ordered the press not to publish a story about a reputed mob boss, but the newspaper ignored the order, printing the story in the next morning's newspaper without making any effort to appeal the order of the trial court. Although the trial court later lifted the restraining order, the editor was found in criminal contempt, the newspaper was fined $100,000, and the editor's eighteen-month sentence was suspended on condition that Hauser perform 200 hours of community service.[43] The federal appellate court reversed the trial court but warned: "A publisher seeking to challenge an order it deems transparently unconstitutional must concern itself with establishing a record of its good faith effort" to lodge an appeal before publishing such material. Indeed,

> It is not asking too much, beyond some additional expense and time, to require a publisher—even when he thinks it is the subject of a transparently unconstitutional order or prior restraint—to make a good faith effort to seek emergency relief from the appellate court. . . . If timely access to the appellate court is not available or if a timely decision is not forthcoming, the publisher may then proceed to publish and challenge the constitutionality of the order.

The federal appellate court was greatly concerned with "the respect owing to court processes."

In England, publications tending to influence the disposition of matters sub judice have long been punished as contempt of court.[44] The English practice prevents newspaper editorials from advocating one or another disposition of a pending case, as well as precluding pre-trial publication of information that might prejudice potential jurors. But in the United States such restraints are rare, though the Supreme Court has admitted that "without some protection for seeking out the news, freedom of the press could be eviscerated."[45] First Amendment rights of the press and media are also intended to preserve the process of self-government, that is, the retention of meaningful control over government through public discussion of its operation, and public officials are constitutionally required to make available information necessary to meaningful discussion about government. The criminal trial is one context in which access is necessary to the achievement of that end of purpose.[46] As stated by the U.S. Supreme Court in Mills v. Alabama,[47] there is "practically universal agreement that a major purpose of the First Amendment was to protect the free discussion of governmental affairs."

Free discussion of governmental affairs was somewhat hampered by the decision of the Federal Communications Commission (FCC) on August 4, 1987, to abolish its "fairness doctrine," which called for equal time in broadcasting for all responsible viewpoints. The FCC determined that the doctrine unconstitutionally restricted the free speech rights of broadcast journalists, at the expense of the print media.[48] Administering the fairness doctrine required the FCC "to second-guess the editorial judgment of broadcasters—first, as to whether a controversial issue of public importance was involved and second as to whether the broadcaster reasonably aired contrasting views."[49] The FCC concluded that the doctrine "did not serve the public interest because the doctrine did, in fact, chill broadcasters," and that the doctrine "fails to meet the test for constitutionality." In the FCC statement, there was an admission that this 1987 ruling was "based on the fact that the doctrine results in excessive and unnecessary Government intervention into the editorial process of broadcast journalists. . . . There is no way for Government to restrict freedom of speech or the press and foster a robust and unfettered exchange of ideas. In short, Government restrictions on speakers' rights injures the public interest."[50]

State courts readily protect freedom of the press by finding First Amendment protections therein. In Associated Press v. Bell,[51] the New York Court of Appeals in 1987 proclaimed that the right of access for the press and the public to criminal trials extends to pre-trial suppression motions, which "frequently challenge the acts of the police and prosecutor . . . giving particular value and significance to conducting such hearings in the public eye."[52] The state court was aware that in its 1980 decision in Richmond Newspapers, Inc. v. Virginia,[53] the U.S. Supreme Court had also recognized the right of access. The highest New York court continued: "A hypothetical risk of prejudice or taint cannot justify categorical denial of public access to suppression hearings because, as a general matter, the important interests of *both* the accused and the public can be accommodated."[54] Thus, the New York trial court had "improperly closed the door on petitioner's First Amendment rights."[55]

The freedom of the press under the First Amendment provides almost an immunity for tort liability, as illustrated by the 1987 New York decision in Daniel v. Dow Jones & Co.[56] Here plaintiff sued the news service for $8,000, alleging that he relied on its report (in his computer) describing the restructuring of Husky Oil, a Canadian corporation; but the report failed to mention that the prices stated were not in U.S. dollars but in Canadian dollars. Plaintiff, believing an $11.80 offer was in U.S. currency, bought 1,230 shares and later sold the shares at a loss. The court held that publishers that provide information to subscribers by computerized news services are entitled to the same First Amendment protections for negligently publishing false or misleading statements as are newspaper publishers or other media providers. According to the court, "Plaintiff provides no reason for treating a person who reads data on a computer screen differently from one who reads it on paper. The potential devastating effects of a holding of liability on a publisher is no different; the potential harm to the free dissemination of news and ideas is the same."

One aspect of freedom of the press and the First Amendment that has caused much consternation in the press are the so-called "shield laws,"[57] i.e., the press and media must have a shield to protect against efforts by government or private persons to extract sources of information; also the press and media demand a sword to defend all their rights under the First Amendment.[58] But the courts have been somewhat reluctant to respect "shield laws," as illustrated in Tofani v. State of Maryland,[59] where the Maryland court permitted disclosure of virtually everything a reporter had learned in the course of gathering a story, confidential or not, if the information went to the heart of a case before the court! The U.S. Supreme Court in 1972 in Branzburg v. Hayes[60] had refused to find constitutional protections for newsmen who had been subpoenaed by grand juries investigating criminal activities.[61] In general, the media-press will be required to disclose information where there is, on balance, a definite need for some third party (including the government) for that information.[62] State "sunshine laws," requiring public bodies to hold open sessions, have made the news-gathering activities of the press and media much easier.[63]

NOTES

1. See generally 26 Ariz L Rev 933 (1984).
2. See Warren Freedman, "News Media Coverage of Criminal Cases and the Right to a Fair Trial," 40 Neb L Rev 391 (1961). Also see In Re Oliver, 333 US 257 (1948).
3. 2 Blackstone Commentaries 373–74 (Kerr ed., 1876).
4. See chapter 1 herein.
5. See State ex rel Herald Mail Co. v. Hamilton, 267 SE2d 544 (W.Va., 1980).
6. 420 US 469 (1975).
7. Id. at pp. 491–92.
8. See State ex rel Daily Mail Publishing Co. v. Smith, 248 SE2d 269 (W.Va., 1978.).
9. 283 US 697 (1931).
10. 402 US 415 (1971). See Editorial, NLJ (June 22, 1987).
11. 403 US 713 (1971).
12. 427 US 539 (1976).

13. 248 NW2d 493 (Iowa, 1976).
14. See 1985 Utah L Rev 739 (1985).
15. 685 F2d 1162 (9th Cir., 1982).
16. Id. at pp. 1167–68.
17. 443 US 368 (1979) at pp. 440 et seq.
18. See generally 59 S Cal L Rev 603 (1986).
19. 139 Ariz 246, 678 P2d 431 (1984).
20. 384 US 333 (1966).
21. See generally 26 Ariz L Rev (1984) at pp. 937–38.
22. 522 F2d 234 (6th Cir., 1975).
23. 695 F2d 1278 (11th Cir., 1983), cert den 461 US 931 (1983) sub nom Post-Newsweek Stations, Florida, Inc. v. United States.
24. See Richmond Newspapers, Inc. v. Virginia, 448 US 555 (1980) at p. 581.
25. 695 F2d 807 (5th Cir., 1982).
26. Id. at p. 810.
27. See Miami Herald Publishing Co. v. Krentzman, 435 US 968 (1978).
28. 373 US 723 (1963.)
29. 384 US 333 (1965); also infra note 14.
30. 366 US 717 (1961).
31. 421 US 794 (1975). Also note State of Utah v. Pierre, 572 P2d 1338 (Utah, 1977), cert den 439 US 882 (1978), for a comparable set of facts.
32. See Kearns-Tribune Corp. v. Lewis, 685 P2d 515 (Utah, 1984).
33. See San Jose-Mercury News v. Municipal Court, 30 Cal3d 498, 638 P2d 655 (1982) and Azbill v. Fisher, 442 P2d 916 (Nev., 1968).
34. 612 P2d 778 (Utah, 1980).
35. Id. at pp. 783–84.
36. Infra note 32.
37. 408 US 665 (1972).
38. Id. at p. 680.
39. 98 NM 261, 648 P2d 300 (1982). See also 14 N.M. L Rev 401 (Spring 1984).
40. Note that the U.S. Supreme Court in its 1981 decision in Chandler v. Florida, 449 US 560 (1981), had upheld the right of the states to experiment with cameras in the courtroom.
41. 97 Wash 2d 30, 640 P2d 716 (1982).
42. ———F2d——— (1st Cir., 1987), Docket 86–1336.
43. See NLJ (June 8, 1987) at p. 14, and NLJ (June 22, 1987) at p. 10.
44. See generally 48 Harv L Rev 885 (1935), and Attorney General v. Times Newspapers, Ltd. (1974) A.C. 173.
45. See Branzburg v. Hayes, 408 US 665 (1972) at p. 681.
46. See 94 Harv L Rev 75 (1980) at p. 151.

47. 384 US 214 (1966) at p. 218.
48. New York Times (Aug. 5, 1987) at pp. 1 et seq.
49. Id. at p. C26.
50. Id. at p. C26.
51. 70 NY2d 32 (1987).
52. Id. at 38.
53. 448 US 555 (1980), aff.
54. Infra note 51 at 38.
55. Id. at 40.
56. ———NYS2d——— (New York County, November 6, 1987).
57. Perhaps 25 States have enacted ''shield'' laws; see 14 Memphis St. U L Rev 418 (1984).
58. Note Case & Comment (November-December 1987) at 16 et seq.
59. 465 A2d 413 (Md., 1983).
60. 408 US 665 (1972).
61. Cf. State of North Carolina v. Hageman, 296 SE2d 433 (N.C., 1982).
62. See CBS, Inc. v. Campbell, 645 SW2d 30 (Mo App., 1982).
63. Infra note 58 at 20 et seq.

3

The Sixth Amendment and the Fair Trial Guarantee

"In all criminal prosecutions, the accused shall enjoy the right to a speedy and public trial, by impartial jury of the State and district wherein the crime shall have been committed," according to the Sixth Amendment to the U.S. Constitution.[1] It is self-evident that the guarantee of a public trial was created for the benefit of the accused defendant, as particularized by the U.S. Supreme Court's decision in Gannett Co. v. DePasquale.[1.1] The guarantee of a public trial for the accused defendant was not designed to protect the public's right to know, for that purpose and goal is delineated under the First Amendment in terms of freedom of speech and of the press.[2] Under the First Amendment, the public and the press have an affirmative constitutional right to attend criminal trials.[3] Press and media coverge of criminal trials is central to the First Amendment, "assuring freedom of communication on matters relating to the functioning of government."[4] It is readily apparent that there is an almost irreconcilable and open conflict between freedom of press and the public trial under the First Amendment and the fair and public trial afforded the accused defendant under the Sixth Amendment. (It should be noted that the Fourteenth Amendment to the U.S. Constitution guarantees those very rights in state court criminal proceedings.)[5]

There are obviously limitations on access by the public and the press and media to a criminal trial, and the right to a fair trial for the accused defendant must be reconciled with this concept of the open and public trial. It is well known that widespread publicity, for example, may prejudice the defendant's right to a fair trial. A survey of recent court decisions sheds light only on the confusion over the issue; few, if any, meaningful guidelines have been evoked by the highest courts.[6] It would appear, however, that there has been an expansion of the public's and the press's and media's rights to public trials at the expense of the accused defendant's right to a fair trial.

Perhaps only the 1966 U.S. Supreme Court decision in Sheppard v. Maxwell[7] gave sufficient sanction to the trial court's utilization of a protective order to ensure protection of the defendant's right to a fair trial: "Given the prevasiveness of modern communications and the difficulty of effacing prejudicial publicity from the minds of the jurors, the trial courts must take strong measures to ensure that the balance is never weighed against the accused." But in 1976, the Court, in Nebraska Press Association v. Stuart,[8] gave its approval to the media's publishing or broadcasting information relating to a defendant's admission of guilt. In Globe Newspaper Co. v. Superior Court,[9] the Court held that the Massachusetts statute that mandated closure of the criminal courtroom during the testimony of minor victims of sexual abuse was unconstitutional under the First Amendment as an abridgement of the guarantee of open and public trial. Little concern was given to the question of fairness of trial for the accused defendant.

In Irvin v. Dowd,[10] the U.S. Supreme Court in 1961 had struck down a conviction by a state court solely on the ground of prejudicial pre-trial publicity. Six murders were committed in the vicinity of the Indiana county, and the defendant had confessed to the six murders and to twenty-four burglaries. There were newspaper reports that the defendant had offered to plead guilty if promised a ninety-nine-year sentence. He was described in newspaper stories as the "confessed slayer of six," a parole violator, and a fraudulent check operator. More than 370 prospective jurors at the voir dire admitted having an opinion as to his guilt. Justice Tom Clark opined:

> It is not required . . . that the jurors be totally ignorant of the facts and issues involved. In these days of swift, widespread and diverse methods of communication, an important case can be expected to arouse the interest of the public in the vicinity, and scarcely any of those best qualified to serve as jurors will not have formed some impression or opinion as to the merits of the case. This is particularly true in criminal cases. To hold that the mere existence of any

preconceived notion as to the guilt or innocence of an accused, without more, is sufficient to rebut the presumption of a prospective juror's impartiality would be to establish an impossible standard. It is sufficient if the juror can lay aside his impression or opinion and render a verdict based on the evidence presented in court.

. . . Here the pattern of deep and bitter prejudice shown to be present throughout the community was clearly reflected in the sum total of the voir dire examination of a majority of the jurors finally placed in the jury box. Eight out of the 12 thought petitioner was guilty. . . . No doubt each juror was sincere when he said that he would be fair and impartial to petitioner, but psychological impact requiring such a declaration before one's fellows is often its father. Where so many, so many times, admitted prejudice, such a statement of impartiality can be given little weight.

Two years later, in Rideau v. Louisiana,[11] the Court observed that weeks before the accused was arraigned on charges of robbery, kidnapping, and murder, the local television station had several times broadcast a twenty-minute film of the defendant flanked by the sheriff and two state troopers, admitting in detail the commission of various offenses in response to leading questions by the sheriff. Justice Potter Stewart declared:

It was a denial of due process of law to refuse the request for a change of venue, after the people of [the] Parish had been exposed repeatedly and in depth to the spectacle of Rideau personally confessing in detail to the crimes with which he was later to be charged. For anyone who has ever watched television the conclusion cannot be avoided that this spectacle, to the tens of thousands of people who saw and heard it, in a very real sense *was* Rideau's trial—at which he pleaded guilty to murder. Any subsequent court proceedings in a community so pervasively exposed to such a spectacle could be but a hollow formality. We do not hesitate to hold, without pausing to examine a particularized transcript of the voir dire examination of the members of the jury, that due process of law in this case required a trial before a jury drawn from a community of people who had not seen and heard Rideau's televised "interview."

In Press Enterprise v. Superior Court,[12] the voir dire examination in a rape and murder trial was declared open to the public and the press and media, despite the argument of the state that the presence of the press would restrict jury candor and also violate the jurors' rights of privacy. Again, the Sixth Amendment right of the accused to a fair trial was not squarely at issue, although the Court opined that "openness . . . enhances both the basic fairness of the criminal trial and the appearance of fairness so essential to public confidence in the system."[13] However, in Waller v. Georgia,[14] the Court demonstrated concern for the accused by holding that a defendant's Sixth Amendment right to a public trial applied to a pre-trial suppression hearing:

> Under the Sixth Amendment any closure of a pre-trial suppression hearing over the objections of the accused must meet the tests set out in Press-Enterprise and its predecessors.[15] . . . There can be little doubt that the explicit Sixth Amendment right of the accused is no less protective of a public trial than the implicit First Amendment right of the press and the public.[16]

In short, public trials promote justice because they enable the public to see that an accused is treated fairly and is not unjustly convicted. Here the defendant had asserted that the Sixth Amendment public trial guarantee was applicable to pre-trial suppression hearings.[17] The Sixth Amendment right was deemed "personal" to the accused and not exercisable independently by the public or the press and media.[18] Indeed, in the Gannett Co. case,[19] the U.S. Supreme Court in 1979 had pointed out that "in the adversary system of criminal justice, the public interest in the administration of justice is protected by the participants in the litigation."[20] Sixth Amendment consideration might prompt a defendant to favor access of the public and press and media and at other times push a defendant to favor closure, as where there is prejudicial adverse publicity or where the incriminating evidence, although inadmissible at trial, might taint the jury pool and threaten the accused's fair trial right.[21]

In a dissenting opinion by Utah Judge Daniels in Kearns-Tribune Corp. v. Lewis,[22] there appears the language that "the Sixth Amendment right to a public trial was intended to guard against 'star chamber' abuses that may result from secret meetings. But news media have no standing to assert this right." The historical accuracy of this averment leaves much to be desired, for the fair trial aspect of the Sixth Amendment necessitates much more than merely a public trial. While it is true that the Sixth Amendment right belongs to the accused, the interest of the public in criminal trials mandates more than the fairness attribute of the Sixth Amendment if the judicial process is to achieve respectability. The U.S. Supreme Court in Gannett Co. v.

DePasquale[23] pointed out that while "a defendant cannot waive a jury trial without the consent of the prosecutor and judge," nevertheless "the public interest is fully protected by the participants in the litigation," though "a member of the public [cannot] demand a jury trial [for the defendant] because of the societal interest in that mode of fact-finding. . . . A member of the general public surely has no right to prevent a continuance in order to vindicate the public interest in the efficient administration of justice." The point is simply that the fairness attribute of the criminal trial inherent in the Sixth Amendment demands confirmation by the right of the public and the press and media in their quest for access to the criminal courtroom. The public and the press and media do not have a Sixth Amendment right to an open or public criminal trial.[24] "The history of the Sixth Amendment totally fails to demonstrate that the Framers of the Sixth Amendment intended to create a constitutional right in strangers to attend a pre-trial proceeding, when all that they actually did was to confer upon the accused an explicit right to demand a public trial. . . . The Sixth Amendment confers the right to a public trial only upon a defendant and only in a criminal case."[25]

It is therefore understandable why pre-trial media coverage that discloses inculpatory, inadmissible evidence to jurors or in-court media conduct that creates a carnival atmosphere in the courtroom has readily brought about reversal of prejudiced criminal convictions.[26] Short of reversal are such alternatives as continuances, transfers, jury sequestration, and new trials. Closure is not a satisfactory remedy, although these remedial measures would be unnecessary if unfair trials did not occur or could be averted.

In addition to the Sixth Amendment on the fair trial guarantee, the Ninth Amendment and the Fourteenth Amendment have a role to play, albeit one of much less of importance. The Ninth Amendment is short and clear: "The enumeration in the Constitution of certain rights shall not be construed to deny or disparage others retained by the people."[27] The Ninth Amendment would favor the right of privacy, for example, and, as the U.S. Supreme Court observed in Richmond Newspapers Inc. v. Virginia,[28] it is the Ninth Amendment's unenumerated rights that enhance the constitutional right of the public to attend trials in the interest of the fair trial. As the highest Court echoed much earlier in the Griswold case,[29] "the Ninth Amendment simply lends strong support to the view that the liberty protected by the Fifth and Fourteenth Amendments from infringement by the federal government or the States is not restricted to rights specifically mentioned in the first eight Amendments.''

The Fourteenth Amendment simply makes the states guarantee all these rights like the federal government does;[30] it was adopted in the era following the Civil War when a demand arose for federal protection of civil rights against encroachment by state governments.[31] It was in 1897 in Allgeyer v. Louisiana[32] that the highest Court revealed its willingness, in dicta, to use the Fourteenth Amendment to place limitations on intrusive actions by state governments. Later in the 1905 landmark case of Lochner v. New York[33] the Court utilized the due process clause of the Fourteenth Amendment to protect property rights by striking down a New York law limiting employment in bakeries to ten hours per day! And in 1925 in United States v. Carolene Products Co.[34] the Court determined that the free speech clause of the First Amendment was applicable to the states by reason of the due process clause of the Fourteenth Amendment.

NOTES

1. See Warren Freedman, The Constitutional Right to a Speedy and Fair Trial (Quorum Books, 1988).

1.1 443 US 368 (1979). See generally 85 Colum L Rev 1546 (1985).

2. See Chapters 1 and 2 herein.

3. See Richmond Newspapers, Inc. v. Virginia, 448 US 555 (1980).

4. Id. at p. 575.

5. ''Nor shall any State deprive any person of life, liberty, or property, without due process of law.''

6. See 59 S Cal L Rev 603 (1986).

7. 384 US 333 (1966).

8. 427 US 539 (1976).

9. 457 US 596 (1982).

10. 366 US 717 (1961).

11. 373 US 723 (1963).

12. 464 US 501 (1984).

13. Id. at p. 508.

14. 104 S Ct 2210 (1984).

15. Id. at p. 2216.

16. Id. at p. 2215.

17. Id. at p. 2214.

18. Infra note 6 at p. 616.

19. Infra note 1.
20. Id. at p. 383.
21. Infra note 6 at p. 622.
22. 685 P2d 515 (Utah, 1984).
23. Infra note 1.
24. Infra note 1.
25. Id. at pp. 385–87.
26. See 19 Suffolk U L Rev 129 (1985).
27. See generally NLJ (January 18, 1988) at 37.
28. 448 US 555 (1979).
29. 381 US 493 (1962).
30. Infra note 5.
31.

No state shall make or enforce any law which shall abridge the privileges or immunities of the citizens of the United States; nor shall the state deprive any person of life, liberty or property without due process of law; nor deny to any person within its jurisdiction the equal protection of the laws.

32. 165 US 578 (1897).
33. 198 US 45 (1905).
34. 304 US 144 (1925).

4

Closure of the Criminal Courtroom

Closure of the criminal courtroom is a drastic remedy even in the face of the accused's clear right under the Sixth Amendment to a fair and public trial.[1] Closure flies squarely in the face of the democratic precepts under the First Amendment in terms of access of the public and the press and media to the criminal courtroom.[2] The U.S. Supreme Court in Gannett Co. v. DePasquale[3] in 1979 set forth two standards to test the appropriateness of any closure of the criminal courtroom: "only where strictly and inescapably necessary to protect the defendant's fair trial guarantee"[4] and "whenever a fair trial for the defendant is likely to be jeopardized by publicity."[5] The latter test delineated by Justice Lewis Powell is less stringent, yet neither test answers the fundamental question as to the nature and the extent of protection to be afforded other parties to the criminal proceeding: the public, the press and media, and the victim of the criminality. The vitality of the First Amendment's vesting access to the criminal courtroom for the public and for the press and media is omitted by these two tests.

The victim of the criminality was the subject of a Massachusetts statute that sought to protect the child-victim of a rape or sexual attack by closing the courtroom to the public and press and media. In Commonwealth v. Aladjem,[6] the 1979 indictments alleged the forcible rape of three minor females; Globe Newspaper Co., in opposing the closure, cited the fact that closure was objected to by the accused and that the prosecutor did not request closure. The criminal trial resulted in acquittal, but the Massachusetts Supreme Judicial Court upheld the closure,[7] based upon the legislative purpose: "to encourage young victims of sexual offenses to come forward; once they come forward, the statute is designed to preserve their ability to testify by protecting them from undue psychological harm at trial." Thus the purpose of the statute was not only to protect juvenile privacy but to promote "sound and orderly administration of justice. . . . We believe that a policy of admitting the press during the young victims' testimony would substantially increase the risk that the Commonwealth would lose the benefit of that testimony."

The U.S. Supreme Court reversed,[8] holding that the mandatory closure rule cannot be justified even in face of the compelling interest in the minor's physical and mental well-being. Justice William Brennan opined that the victim's attempt to express to the public "precisely what a heinous crime the defendant had committed" would be thwarted by the mandatory closure provision of the Massachusetts statute.[9] Justice Brennan did note that the trial judge had discretion to prevent newpaper reporters, for example, from confronting or questioning the minor victim. But there was no empirical evidence supporting the claim that the statute would lead to an increase in number of rape victims coming forward to testify. Accordingly, the statute violated the First Amendment since Massachusetts's interests were neither sufficiently tailored nor sufficiently compelling.[10] The dissenting opinion of Chief Justice Burger (joined by Justice William Rehnquist) argued that society has historically gone to great pains to protect minors charged with crimes: It would misrepresent the historical record to state that there is an unbroken, uncontradicted history of open proceedings in cases involving the sexual abuse of minors." The dissent saw the controversy as purely between "the interests of the media for instant access against the interest of the State in protecting child rape victims from the trauma of public testimony." The dissent pointed out that the press and the public did have complete access to the victim's testimony subsequently: "Paradoxically the court denies the victims the kind of protection routinely given to juveniles who commit crimes."[11]

The juvenile court system in the United States has traditionally shielded offenders from the public gaze.[12] The rationale for such closure is that youthful offenders should be rehabilitated, not punished, and therefore harsh publicity in the press or media would be detrimental to such treatment. It is said that juvenile courts reach back to the tenth century,[13] but in the early nineteenth century, it was clearly seen that juveniles should not be treated like adults and jailed along with hardened criminals.[14] Segregation of youthful offenders prompted the building in 1825 of the New York House of Refuge[15] under a state legislature grant for children who had committed minor offenses and who were considered somewhat innocent of criminal ways.[16] As an alternative to incarceration, the house was, at most, a humanitarian gesture and not a concrete corrective measure. Soon similar juvenile homes were established throughout the country, with the emphasis on creating a family life for juvenile offenders.

In 1889, the Illinois Juvenile Court Act[17] established the first statewide forum for hearing delinquency, dependency, and neglect proceedings involving children. The Illinois court system featured confidential records, private hearings, and procedural informality for youthful offenders.[18] The doctrine of parens patriae was then implanted in the legal system, so that the state, being deeply concerned with dependent and neglected juveniles,[19] could intervene to furnish parental care and even control. Children were no longer treated as criminals but would receive treatment and precious concern in the juvenile court.

The promulgation of similar laws gave rise to litigation challenging their constitutionality on grounds that these laws failed to comply with the Seventh Amendment's guarantee of trial by jury,[20] the Fourteenth Amendment's guarantee of due process of law,[21] and the right of the accused to be confronted with witnesses.[22] But in Commonwealth v. Fisher,[23] the Pennsylvania court, like most other courts, upheld these juvenile court laws against nonconstitutionality:

> To save a child from becoming a criminal, or from continuing in a career of crime, to end in maturer years in public punishment and disgrace, the Legislature surely may provide for the salvation of such a child, if its parents or guardians be unable or unwilling to do so, by bringing it into one of the courts of the state without any process at all, for the purpose of subjecting it to the state's guardianship and protection. The natural parent needs no process to temporarily deprive his child of its liberty by confining it in his own home, to save it and to shield it from the consequences of persistence in a career of waywardness; nor is the state, when compelled, as *parens patriae,* to take the place of the father for the same purpose, required to adopt any process as a means of placing its hands upon the child to lead it into one of its courts.[24]

The U.S. Supreme Court in its 1967 decision in In Re Gault[25] swept aside much of the informality in juvenile hearings by introducing guidelines for due process of law and less informality in the juvenile courtroom so as to conform to the constitutional mode.

Most states today have mechanisms by which the juvenile court judge can prohibit the press or media from publishing information concerning delinquency hearings or proceedings.[26] Juvenile courts have indeed barred the press and media from the courtroom.[27] In Oklahoma Publishing Co. v. District Court,[28] the name and picture of an eleven year old charged with murder was obtained when the child appeared at a pre-trial detention hearing. The press was present with the knowledge of the prosecutor, the defense counsel, and the judge. A number of stories using the boy's name and picture were printed in the newspaper and broadcast on television until the juvenile court entered an order prohibiting further publication, and the Oklahoma Supreme Court upheld the restraining order. But the U.S. Supreme Court reversed on the ground that the juvenile court had assented to the press and media's being in the juvenile courtroom. Indeed press and media access enables the public to know about the activities of its juvenile courts and to evaluate their work based on concrete information. Access can also aid the juvenile court by focusing attention on their limited and inadequate resources.[29]

It would appear that juvenile courts can still protect juveniles in need of anonymity by refusing to release names rather than by closing the doors of the juvenile courtroom. In RLR v. State of Alaska,[30] the Alaskan court ruled that juveniles had the right to a public trial. In Brian W. v. Superior Court,[31] the California court admitted the news media to a hearing of a seventeen year old charged with grand theft, robbery, kidnapping, and murder, although the juvenile statute excluded the public from the hearing, except for persons whom the judge deemed "to have a direct and legitimate interest in the particular case or in the work of the court." The California Supreme Court upheld the trial court's discretion by emphasizing the role of the press and media in "encouraging the fairness of trials and subjecting the administration of justice to the beneficial effects of public scrutiny."

In 1982, the *Columbia Journal of Law and Social Problems,*[32] after a lengthy study of the problem, recommended that juvenile hearings be open to the press and media for general reporting, unless there are unusual or exceptional circumstances, and they offered the following model statute:

> (1) The general public shall be excluded, and only parties, their counsel, witnesses, and other persons whom the court finds to have a legitimate interest in the case or in the work of the court may be admitted by the court. Representatives of the media shall be admitted by the court, unless the court makes a preliminary determination pursuant to subsection (2) of this section.
>
> (2) Prior to the initial hearing in the case, the child may request the court to exclude the media from any hearing in the case. The court may so exclude the media only if it determines that it is in the best interests of the child that he or she remains anonymous and that anonymity is unlikely to be preserved without such exclusion. If the court decides to exclude, the media may challenge the decision before the court prior to the initial hearing.
>
> (3) Prior to the initial hearing, the court shall make a determination as to whether the name of the child and/or other personal information that might identify the child may be disseminated by the media. The only identifying material which may be disseminated is that which concerns a child *14 years of age or older,* previously adjudicated a delinquent, and charged with an offense involving *serious property damage, manufacture or distribution of a narcotic drug, or violence to the person, or an offense which, if committed by an adult, would constitute murder or manslaughter*. The court shall permit public dissemination of such information when to do so would be in the best interests of the child in his or her rehabilitation and in the best interests of the public. Prior to the hearing, the court shall communicate such determination to those representatives of the media who wish to have access to the hearing. Representatives of the media who, nevertheless, publish such prohibited information shall be subject to a fine of $________. Violation of this statute shall be deemed a Class ________ Misdemeanor.
>
> (4) This section shall apply to both adjudicatory and dispositional hearings.[33]

Closure of the courtroom in nonjuvenile court proceedings is less readily obtained, as illustrated in Matter of the Applications of the Associated Press, et al. v. Bell[34] in which newspapers and television stations petitioned the court to avoid closure in a criminal trial. It was the accused who sought and was granted closure based on the argument that publicity with respect to the evidence (which may be suppressed) would violate his Sixth Amendment rights to a fair trial. The New York Appellate Division, First Department, in granting the petition, found that the trial court order, excluding the public and the press from the pre-trial suppression hearing relating to the admissibility of videotaped and written statements made by the accused after his arrest, had violated the rights guaranteed to the public and to the press and media by the First and Fifth amendments of the U.S. Constitution and Article I, section 8 of the New York State Constitution. Closure was not justified by the possible adverse publicity.

On June 9, 1987, the New York Court of Appeals unanimously agreed that the First Amendment protects an affirmative right of access by the public and the press to criminal hearings, including pre-trial suppression hearings.[35] Only eight years earlier in 1979, in Gannett v. DePasquale,[36] the same court had upheld closed proceedings (in a divided ruling), a vote upheld by the U.S. Supreme Court.[37] (The Gannett case dealt with a pre-trial supression hearing, that is, a proceeding to determine if certain evidence can properly be heard by a jury.) In 1954, the New York Court of Appeals, in United Press Association v. Valente,[38] had ruled that no enforceable right of public access to court proceedings exists under the First Amendment. However, the four dissenters of the U.S. Supreme Court in the Gannett case affirmance[39] had stated that they would require ''an accused who seeks closure to establish that it is strictly and inescapably necessary in order to protect the fair trial guarantee.''[40] Justice Blackmun (one of the dissenters) urged that the Sixth Amendment bars closure of a suppression hearing unless there was demonstrated a ''substantial probability that irreparable damage to defendant's fair trial right will result from conducting the proceeding in public . . . [that] alternatives to closure will not work, and [that closure] will be effective in protecting against the perceived harm.''[41]

In 1980 in Richmond Newspapers Inc. v. Virginia,[42] the highest Court, in a 7-2 decision, had recognized an affirmative, constitutionally protected right of the public and press to attend criminal proceedings. Chief Justice Burger wrote that ''people sensed from experience and observation that, especially in the administration of criminal justice, the means used to achieve justice must have support derived from public acceptance of both the process and its results.''[43] In 1982 in Globe Newspaper Co. v. Superior Court,[44] the U.S. Supreme Court struck down a Massachusetts statute that required all trials involving underage victims of sexual offenses to be closed to the public. In Press-Enterprise Co. v. Supreme Court[45] in 1984, the Court opined that the

First Amendment created a presumption in favor of public access to jury selection; and in 1986 in Press-Enterprise Co. v. Superior Court of California,[46] the closure of a preliminary hearing was held to be unconstitutional by the highest Court.

The New York Court of Appeals decision in 1987 in the Associated Press v. Bell[47] concluded that a pre-trial suppression hearing cannot be properly closed unless and until a court made explicit findings that there would be substantial probability of prejudice to the criminal defendant's rights, that there were no reasonable alternatives to closure, and that closure would in effect safeguard against the demonstrated risk.

In Re Petition of the Daily Item,[48] the Pennsylvania court ruled that a trial court must consider fully the public's right of access to the preliminary hearing before it can order closure of the criminal courtroom. (The trial court also had impounded a stenographic transcript of the proceeding.) The trial court had erred in believing that the preliminary hearing was not a criminal trial to which the right of access attached. The preliminary hearing was an adjudicative criminal proceeding designed to prevent unlawful detention. The public as well as the press and media had an interest in this proceeding, a stage of the criminal process. The defendant here failed to show a "serious threat" to his right to a fair trial so as to justify closure; there was no "clear and present danger" to defendant's right to a fair trial.[49] And in Commonwealth v. Hayes,[50] the Pennsylvania court held that closure may not be ordered where there is some other procedural device to protect the defendant's right to a fair trial.

An Arkansas judge had closed the evidence suppression hearing to the public and press and media where the defendant was charged with raping and murdering a nurse. In Arkansas Television Co. v. Tedder,[51] closure was contested, especially since the trial judge who stated that the contents of the hearing would not be disclosed until the "probable prejudicial effect of public disclosure . . . no longer existed." The Arkansas Supreme Court, long after the trial itself had concluded, found that the trial court had erred.[52]

A distinctly popular view was taken by the Third U.S. Court of Appeals in its 1949 decision in United States v. Kobli:[53] "Whatever may have been the view of an earlier and more formally modest age, we think that the franker and more realistic attitude of the present day toward matters of sex precludes a determination that all members of the public, the mature and the experienced, as well as the immature and impressionable, may reasonably be excluded from the trial of a sexual offense upon the ground of public morals."

NOTES

1. See Chapter 3 herein.
2. See Chapters 1 and 2 herein.
3. 443 US 368 (1979).
4. Id. at p. 440.
5. Id.
6. 379 Mass 846, 401 NE2d 360 (1979) sub nom Globe Newspaper Co. v. Superior Court.
7. 383 Mass 838, 423 NE2d 773 (1981).
8. 457 US 596 (1982).
9. See generally 11 Hastings Const L Q 637 (Summer 1984).
10. Infra note 8 at pp. 610–11.
11. Id. at p. 612.
12. See generally 17 Colum J L & Soc Probs 287 (1982) at 287.
13. See 1958 Wash U L Q 123 (1958).
14. See 41 Minn L Rev 547 (1957).
15. Infra note 12 at 289–90.
16. See 22 Stan L Rev 1187 (1970).
17. Infra note 12 at 290; also Act of April 21, 1899, Ill Laws at 131.
18. See 30 Rocky Mtn L Rev 101 (1957).
19. Infra note 12 at 291.
20. See, for example, United States ex rel Yonick v. Briggs, 266 Fed 434 (WD Pa., 1920).
21. See Marlowe v. Commonwealth of Kentucky, 133 SW 1137 (Ky., 1911).
22. See Cinque v. Boyd, 121 A 678 (Conn., 1923).
23. 62 A 198 (Pa., 1905).
24. Id. at 200.
25. Note Lindsay v. Lindsay, 100 NE 892 (Ill., 1913) and State v. Burnett, 102 SE 711 (N.C., 1920).
26. See sec. 741 of the New York Family Court Act and also sec. 676 of the California Welfare and Institutions Act, for example.
27. Note sec. 8–235 of Ariz Rev Stats and sec. 16.1–162 of Va Code, for example.
28. 430 US 308 (1977).
29. Infra note 12 at 339.
30. 487 P2d 27 (Alas., 1971).
31. 574 P2d 788 (Cal., 1978).

32. See 17 Colum J L & Soc Probs 287 (1982) for an excellent examination of the entire problem.
33. Id. at 345–46.
34. ———Ad2d———, ———NYS2d——— (1st Dept, May 13, 1987).
35. ———NY2d———, ———NE2d——— (June 9, 1987).
36. 43 NY2d 370, 372 NE2d 544 (1979).
37. 443 US 368 (1979).
38. 308 NY 71 (1954). See generally NYLJ (June 29, 1987) at pp. 1 et seq.
39. Infra note 37.
40. Id. at p. 440.
41. Id. at pp. 441–42.
42. 448 US 555 (1980).
43. Id. at pp. 570–71.
44. 457 US 596 (1982).
45. 464 US 501 (1984).
46. 106 S Ct 2735 (1986).
47. Infra note 35.
48. 456 A2d 580 (Pa., 1980); see also 23 Duq L Rev 293 (1984).
49. See Commonwealth v. Klinger, 75 Pa D & C2d 664 (1976).
50. 489 Pa 419, 414 A2d 318 (1980), cert den 449 US 992 (1981).
51. 281 Ark 152, 662 SW2d 174 (1983).
52. See generally 38 Ark L Rev 403 (1984).
53. 172 F2d 919 (3d Cir., 1949).

5

Photographing, Broadcasting, and Televising in the Criminal Courtroom

The First and the Sixth amendments to the U.S. Constitution, buttressed by the Fourteenth Amendment with respect to states, mandate a public trial for criminal defendants, as well as access to the criminal courtroom by the public and by the press and media.[1] Since the founding of the United States, the press and media have attended and reported on criminal trial proceedings, from a reporter's prose description to an artist's sketch pad rendition and then progressing to the still camera, to the movie camera with its bright lights, and finally to the modern, portable video camera.[2]

Photography brought to the press and media the opportunity to give the public an intimate view of criminal justice in action. From the outset, however, there was concern about the impact of such sensationalized and perhaps prejudicial press coverage on the accused's Sixth Amendment right to a fair trial.[3] In 1917 the Illinois Supreme Court in People v. Munday[4] advised trial courts in Illinois against approving still photography, including newsreel photography, in the criminal courtroom because it was "not in keeping with the dignity a court should maintain, or with the proper and orderly conduct of its business."[5] But the innovative scientific improvement of cameras prompted other state courts to tailor restrictions on photography in the criminal courtroom to fit particular criminal proceedings.[6] The American Bar Association (ABA) in 1931 opined that "photographing of scenes within a courtroom ought not to be permitted."[7] And in 1937, after a series of raucous publicity circuses during criminal trials that outraged the sense of decency of bench and bar,[8] the ABA adopted Canon 35 of its Canons of Judicial Ethics. This dogmatic statement of principles barred newspaper photographers as well as broadcasters and televisers from criminal court proceedings. Canon 35, as amended in 1952 to include television, read as follows:

> Proceedings in court should be conducted with fitting dignity and decorum. The taking of photographs in the court room, during sessions of the court or recesses between sessions, and the broadcasting or televising of court proceedings are calculated to detract from the essential dignity of the proceedings, distract the witness in giving testimony, degrade the court, and create misconceptions with respect thereto in the mind of the public and should not be permitted.

The lone exceptions were ''broadcasting or televising, under the supervision of the court'' of ''such portions of naturalization proceedings [other than the interrogation of applicants] as are designed and carried out exclusively as a ceremony for the purpose of publicly demonstrating in an impressive manner the essential dignity and the serious nature of naturalization.''

The press and media were aroused by what they termed interference with their First Amendment right of freedom of press. They contended that photographing, broadcasting, and televising can be done unobtrusively in the courtroom with modern, versatile camera equipment carrying no flashbulbs or bright lights that might interfere with court proceedings. In 1946 the federal courts were subjected to Rule 53 of the Federal Rules of Criminal Procedure: ''The taking of photographs in the court room during the progress of judicial proceedings or radio broadcasting of judicial proceedings from the court room shall not be permitted by the court.'' (In 1962 the Judicial Conference of the United States extended Rule 53 to ban television also from the federal courts.)[9]

Probably the first live telecast of a criminal court trial occurred on December 13, 1953, in an Oklahoma City court. In State v. Manley,[10] television cameras were housed in a specially constructed booth in the rear of the courtroom. Sound was recorded by a microphone hidden near the front of the court, and additional, unobtrusive lighting was provided by photo-floodlights placed in the chandeliers. Only the swearing of the jurors, part of the trial testimony, and the sentencing of the criminal defendant were televised subsequently during news broadcasts by the local Oklahoma television station. Judge A. P. Van Meter had a small button fastened to his desk that he could push any time he wanted to discontinue the operation of the television cameras. The success of this operation was followed by the telecast from a balcony in the courtroom of the Washburn murder trial[11] in Waco, Texas, on December 6, 1955. On April 7, 1956, despite the affidavit of the accused who was charged with dynamiting an airplane in flight and who objected to television and radio coverage of his criminal trial, a Colorado district court permitted television stations to make sound-on-film movies for later telecasting and permitted radio stations to tape-record for later broadcasting of the criminal proceedings.

It was on September 3, 1958, that solid support for televising criminal proceedings occurred as the Oklahoma Court of Criminal Appeals in Lyles v. State[12] upheld television coverage of the criminal court proceedings on the single ground that a criminal trial is a "public event." The defendant, who received a fifteen-year sentence for burglary, had contended that the television cameras prevented him from getting a fair trial. But the court disagreed, stating that the doors of the court must be kept open to the press and media "to report courtroom abuses, evil and corrupt influences which despoil and stagnate the flow of equal and exact justice."[13] It emphasized that the photographing, broadcasting, and televising of the criminal trial were at all times within the sound discretion of the trial judge, subject to certain general standards of dignity and decorum. Justice Brett took the occasion to label Canon 35 as an "unwarranted presumption" and intimated that the ABA had no right to legislate or to dictate policy to the courts: "When abuses of discretion occur, we in Oklahoma will meet them on appeal and not in a manner of preconception."[14]

The U.S. Supreme Court in 1947 in Craig v. Harney[15] had observed that a criminal trial is a public event, that what transpires in the courtroom is public property, that those who see and hear what transpires may report it with impunity, and that there is no special prerequisite of the judiciary that enables it, as distinguished from other institutions of government, to suppress, edit, or censor public events that transpire before it. Federal district court Judge Gourley in 1957, however, expressed these reservations:

The very thought of members of the press and/or amateur photographers and others employing cameras, no matter how silent and concealed, to photograph different parties and witnesses to a court proceeding while the parties and the court are engrossed in the determination of matters of tremendous moment to the parties involved, is repugnant to the high standard of judicial decorum to which our courts are accustomed, and, indeed, may prove an opening wedge to a gradual deterioration of the judicial process. . . . The greatest danger to freedom may well stem from those who seek license and luxury of increased liberties at the expense of the processes which feed life blood to our free institutions.[16]

Canon 35 was replaced in 1979 by Canon 3A(7), which eliminated some of the rhetoric but not the sting: "A judge should prohibit broadcasting, televising, recording, or taking photographs in the courtroom and areas immediately adjacent thereto during sessions of the court or recesses between sessions." Electronic equipment is permitted in the courtroom but only for "purposes of judicial administration," such as videotapes of depositions by the parties and perpetuation of the record, for "investigative, ceremonial, or naturalization proceedings," and for "instructional purposes in educational institutions."[17] The impact of the opposition to photographing, broadcasting, and televising of criminal trials by the ABA, by the federal court system, and perhaps by a slim majority of states has clouded and unduly complicated public policy considerations and such constitutional guarantees as set forth in the First Amendment,[18] the Sixth Amendment,[19] the Fourteenth Amendment,[20] the Fifth Amendment[21] and even in the constitutional protection of the right of privacy.[22]

The 1965 decision of the U.S. Supreme Court in Estes v. Texas[23] and 1981 decision of the U.S. Supreme Court in Chandler v. Florida[24] each shed their particular light on the problem. The Estes case delineated a circus-like atmosphere created by broadcasters in the criminal courtroom, leaving the highest Court with no alternative other than reversal of the conviction of defendant for swindling due to lack of due process of law under the Fourteenth Amendment. As many as twelve cameras were present at the pre-trial Estes hearing on the defense motion to exclude all cameras from the criminal courtroom: "Cables and wires were snaked across the courtroom floor, three microphones were on the judge's bench and others were beamed at the jury box and the counsel table."[25] During the subsequent trial, the television cameras and the photographers were confined to a booth constructed in the rear of the courtroom; only the opening and closing arguments of the state and the jury verdict were recorded. Nevertheless, the U.S. Supreme Court in a 5-4 vote held in 1965 that the mere presence of television in the criminal courtroom involved such a high probability of prejudice to the accused defendant that no specific prejudice needed to be demonstrated. The conscious or unconscious effect of the televised proceedings on the jurors ''cannot be evaluated, but experience indicates that it is not only possible but highly probable that it will have a direct bearing on his vote as to guilt or innocence.''[26] The effect on the testimony of witnesses was summarized: ''Some may be demoralized and frightened, some cocky and given to overstatement; memories may falter, as with anyone speaking publicly, and accurately [sic] of statement may be severely undermined.''[27] The televising was also believed ''to further political objectives'' of the trial judge and the attorneys.[28] The defendant, Estes, according to the Court, was also a victim of the televising: ''Its presence is a form of mental, if not physical, harassment, resembling a police line-up or the third degree.''[29] The dissent of Justice Stewart pointed out that the trial record did not reveal a physical disruption of the courtroom by the presence of television cameras, nor were the participants televised against their objections.[30] But the majority opinion written by Justice Clark contended that photographic coverage of criminal trials is per se unconstitutional since it ''involves such a probability that prejudice will result that it is deemed inherently lacking in due process.''[31] The decision in Estes v. Texas[32] prompted every state except Colorado to ban televising of criminal trials.[33]

In 1981 the U.S. Supreme Court decided Chandler v. Florida,[34] a case that arose from burglary charges brought against two Miami Beach, Florida, police officers whose incriminating conversation had been intercepted by a ham operator. During the trial, only the testimony of the state's chief witness (the ham operator) and the closing argument of the state were televised by one television camera. The Supreme Court at the outset abandoned any notion that television coverage was per se unconstitutional. Noting the absence of ''empirical data sufficient to establish that the mere presence of broadcast media inherently has an adverse effect,''[35] it ruled that television coverage had not affected the defendants' right to a fair trial. Furthermore, the burden of proof rests on the accused defendants to show specifically how the presence of cameras had violated their due process rights.[36] Thus, in upholding the convictions of the defendants, the Court adopted a states' right position concerning the broadcasting and telecasting of criminal trials. This position, which neither favors nor opposes such coverages, is consonant with notions of federalism, for it calls for experimentation on the part of the several states. Unfortunately, the Court did not entertain discussion of First Amendment values that are necessarily inherent in the concept of the public trial.

It would appear that today perhaps forty-four states permit television coverage of criminal trials either on an experimental or a permanent basis.[37] The states of Indiana, Michigan, Mississippi, Missouri, South Carolina, South Dakota, and Virginia and the District of Columbia prohibit any extended media coverage.[38] The state of Arizona, for example, for the first time permitted gavel-to-gavel coverage of a murder trial between February and May 1987.[39] While the trial judge apparently approved of the successful trial, the defense attorney opined that television coverage "never works to the benefit of a defendant." Viewer reaction was assessed by the Journalism Department of the University of Arizona in 1,000 questionnaires sent to cablevision subscribers, and, although the response was about 25 percent only, it was apparent that almost 94 percent of viewers watched the trial proceedings more than once. About 84 percent of the viewers agreed with the guilty verdict returned by the jury.[40]

Effective December 1, 1987, in the state of New York, audiovisual coverage of criminal trials was authorized for an experimental period of eighteen months.[41] Only selected courtrooms will be permitted access to cameras and to television equipment; the chief administrator of the courts in New York must, inter alia, promulgate a list of acceptable television equipment models that can be used in the coverage of court proceedings.[42] For the still photographer, no more than two cameras "with no more than two lenses for each camera" will be permitted.[43] The New York statute gives the trial judge full discretion to allow or to prohibit such coverages by still photography or by television and/or radio coverage. The trial judge, however, must take into consideration in his or her ruling whether such coverage would interfere with any law enforcement activity, would involve lewd or scandalous matters, would generally interfere with the fair administration of justice, and would not advance the fair trial of the rights of the parties.[44] Under the New York law, the still photographer and/or the media (radio and television) must file a written request with the presiding judge prior to the commencement of the proceeding.[45] If permission is denied, the press or media may file an appeal.[46] Of the many restraints on press and media coverage in New York, the most important are to the effect that members of the jury,[47] participants in the voir dire,[48] and witnesses who are undercover police officers[49] cannot be photographed or televised.

No sooner was the ink dry on the New York "experimental" program than the issue of television coverage was raised in the criminal trial of white defendants accused of a racial attack upon blacks in Howard Beach, Queens. The trial judge on November 24, 1987, denied a request by news organizations to allow television and still cameras at the trial beginning December 1, 1987: "This case is too highly sensitive to be the subject of the media's experimental coverage." The court pointed out that "occasional emotional outbursts" by spectators at the trial "will only exacerbate an already delicate situation . . . and would result in a disruption to the routine that this court has so carefully attempted to set for the jurors."[50] However, an administrative judge on December 4, 1987 overruled the trial judge;[51] the reversal was based upon the reasoning that it was "inappropriate to suggest that the trial is open when only a portion of the media is permitted access." But the New York Appellate Division, 2nd Dept., on December 7, 1987 reversed and ruled that television and newspaper still cameras would not be allowed, even to cover the closing arguments. The higher court found that the trial judge did not abuse his discretion in barring access to television and still cameras, but that the administrative judge had erred in "substituting his discretion for that of the trial judge."[52] In another murder trial, the New York Appellate Division, 1st Dept., on January 21, 1988, upheld a ruling by the trial court that, despite New York's eighteen-month experiment allowing television cameras and microphones into courtrooms, electronic coverage of the criminal trial would not be permitted.[53] Indeed, the trial judge "is expressly accorded broad authority . . . to deny, in his sound discretion, audio-visual coverage in the criminal trial over which he presides." On the other hand, in Matter of An Application to Conduct Visual Coverage of People v. Larry Davis,[54] the New York Supreme Court, Bronx County, in 1988 agreed to allow television coverage because none of the parties objected to camera coverage, provided that the media stayed within the strict guidelines set by the court to maintain demeanor and security in the courtroom.[55]

There is no uniform set of guidelines for televising criminal trials, although the University of Michigan Law Review[56] in December 1985 set forth proposed model guidelines. (See the Appendix following this chapter.) It would be observed that Rule 53 of the Federal Rules of Criminal Procedure still bans television from all federal court criminal trials, despite a defendant's request that his trial be televised, as illustrated by United States v. Hastings,[57] where the federal appellate court ruled that the First Amendment right of access to criminal trials did not include a right to cover criminal trials with audio and video equipment and that the prohibition on such equipment did not violate the First Amendment.[58] The 1981 U.S. Supreme Court decision in Chandler v. Florida[59] undoubtedly brought about the 1982 revision by the ABA of Canon 3A(7), which today reads as follows:

> A judge should prohibit broadcasting, televising, recording or photographing in courtrooms and areas immediately adjacent thereto during sessions of court, or recesses between sessions, except that under rules prescribed by a supervising appellate court or other appropriate authority, a judge may authorize broadcasting, televising, recording and photographing of judicial proceedings in courtrooms and areas immediately adjacent thereto, consistent with the right of the parties to a fair trial and subject to express conditions, limitations, and guidelines which allow such coverage in a manner that will be unobtrusive, will not distract the trial participants, and will not otherwise interfere with the administration of justice.

The ABA ban is still evident, although some latitude or discretion is given to the ''supervising appellate court or other appropriate authority,'' which would sanction television of criminal trials within state courts.

States have indeed exercised that sound discretion over the years, as evidenced by People v. Hagan,[60] where the New York court excluded spectators due to a witness's justifiable fear of reprisal for testifying against the alleged murderers of Malcolm X; by State v. Smith,[61] where the Arizona court excluded spectators during the rape victim's testimony to prevent embarassment and emotional disturbance to the rape victim; and by State v. Santos,[62] where the Rhode Island court, for similar reasons, excluded spectators while a witness testified to details of a sexual assault.

Protection of the right of privacy has been raised as justification for limiting the televising of criminal trials.[63] Courts must avoid public documentation or other exposure of private information; they must "weigh the interests in privacy with the interests of the public to know and of the press to publish."[64] The examples of such sound discretion are legion, as illustrated by the closing of the courtroom during the testimony of an undercover agent,[65] the exclusion of the public during testimony of a teenage pregnant mother based on concern for the welfare of the mother and her unborn child,[66] and exclusion of all spectators except family, close friends, and members of the press and bar in a trial for rape of a nine-year-old girl in which the witnesses were girls of seven and eleven years of age.[67] The Arizona Code of Judicial Conduct Canon 3A(7)(b)(ii) expressly states that the right of privacy of trial participants must be taken into consideration before sanctioning televising of criminal trials.

It was the 1965 decision of the U.S. Supreme Court in Griswold v. Connecticut[68] that elevated the right of privacy to its lofty stature as an independent constitutional right, protecting against public disclosure of private facts; intrusion into another's physical solitude or seclusion; placing a person in a "false light" before the public; and appropriation of another's private name or likeness.[69] But court decisions restraining the press and media from reporting public trials have generally not been concerned per se with possible violations of the right of privacy.[70]

Still another possible limitation on televising criminal trials relates to a defendant's constitutional right to evidence under the Sixth Amendment's compulsory process clause and the Fourteenth Amendment's due process clause.[71] If the presence of television cameras in the criminal courtroom inhibits witnesses, the defendant's ability to obtain evidence is indeed impaired.[72] Accordingly, the right to evidence can be a compelling rationale for limiting camera coverage of criminal trials. Increased publicity and loss of anonymity can play havoc with evidentiary testimony of witnesses, as well as of parties to the litigation. The presence of a camera might even cause witnesses and parties to alter the content of their testimony.[73]

NOTES

1. See Chapters 1–4 herein.
2. See generally 85 Colum L Rev 1546 (1985).

3. See Chapter 3 herein.

4. 280 Ill 32, 117 NE 286 (1917).

5. Id. at pp. 67, 300.

6. See 63 Judicature (June-July 1979) at pp. 14–16.

7. 56 ABA Report 536 (1931).

8. See Warren Freedman, ''News Media Coverage of Criminal Cases and the Right to a Fair Trial,'' 40 Neb L Rev 391 (1961) at p. 400.

9. (1962) Jud Conf Ann Rep 9–10.

10. Dkt. No. 22092, Okla County Dist Ct.

11. See Ex Parte Washburn, 161 Tex Crim 651, 280 SW2d 257 (1955) and Washburn v. State, 164 Tex Crim 448, 299 SW2d 706 (1957).

12. 330 P2d 734 (Okla., 1958); also infra note 8 at p. 404.

13. Id. at p. 740.

14. Id. at pp. 742, 745.

15. 331 US 367 (1947).

16. Tribune Review Publishing Co. v. Thomas, 153 F Supp 486 (WD Pa., 1957) at p. 494.

New York State sec. 52 of the civil rights law has banned photography, broadcasting, and televising in the criminal courtroom since 1952: ''No person, firm, association or corporation shall televise, broadcast, take motion pictures or arrange for the televising, broadcasting or taking of motion pictures within this State of proceedings, in which the testimony of witnesses by subpoena or other compulsory process is or may be taken, conducted by a court, commission, committee, administrative agency, or other tribunal in this State. Any violation of this section shall be a misdemeanor.'' However, in 1987, more than thirty-five years later, the New York legislature passed an amendment providing for the use of cameras in New York courtrooms on an eighteen-month experimental basis beginning December 1, 1987. See NYLJ (May 6, 1987, and June 3, 1987) at p. 1. While giving trial judges discretion to supervise audio-visual coverage, the new law prohibits coverage of trial testimony by covert or undercover police officers without their consent and furthermore prohibits coverage of jurors and victims of sex offenses.

17. See generally 4 U Haw L Rev 85 (1982).

18. See Chapters 1 and 2 herein.

19. See Chapter 3 herein.

20. Both equal protection of the law and the due process of law aspects are touched upon in Chapter 3 herein.

21. The due process of law clause in the Fifth Amendment, in particular.

22. See Warren Freedman, The Right of Privacy in the Computer Age (Quorum Books, 1987).

23. 381 US 532 (1965).

24. 449 US 560 (1981).

25. Infra note 23 at p. 536.
26. Id. at p. 545.
27. Id. at p. 547.
28. Id. at p. 548, Justice Clark wrote:

The State [contends] that the use of television in the instant case was ''without injustice to the person immediately concerned,'' basing its position on the fact that the petitioner has established no isolatable prejudice and that this must be shown in order to invalidate a conviction in these circumstances. . . . It is true that in most cases involving claims of due process deprivations we require a showing of identifiable prejudice to the accused. Nevertheless, at times a procedure employed by the State involves such a probabililty that prejudice will result that it is deemed inherently lacking in due process. The chief function of our judicial machinery is to ascertain the turth. The use of television, however, cannot be said to contribute materially to this objective. Rather its use amounts to the interjection of an irrelevant factor into court proceedings. In addition experience teaches that there are numerous situations in which it might cause actual unfairness—some so subtle as to defy detection by the accused or control by the judge. We enumerate some in summary:

1. The potential impact of television on the jurors is perhaps of the greatest significance. They are the nerve center of the fact-finding process. It is true that in states like Texas where they are required to be sequestered in trials of this nature, the jurors will probably not see any of the proceedings as televised from the courtroom. But the inquiry cannot end there. From the moment the trial judge announces that a case will be televised it becomes a cause célèbre. The whole community, including prospective jurors, becomes interested in all the morbid details surrounding it. . . . Moreover, while it is practically impossible to assess the effect of television on jury attentiveness, those of us who know juries realize the problem of jury ''distraction.'' The State argues this is de minimis since the physical disturbances have been eliminated. But we know that distractions are not caused solely by the physical presence of the camera and its telltale red lights. It is the awareness of the fact of telecasting that is felt by the jurors throughout the trial. . . .

2. The quality of the testimony in criminal trials will often be impaired. The impact upon a witness of the knowledge that he is being viewed by a vast audience is simply incalculable . . . Embarrassment may impede the search for the truth, as may a natural tendency toward overdramatization. . . .

3. A major aspect of the problem is the additional responsibilities the presence of television places on the trial judge. His job is to make certain that the accused receives a fair trial. This most difficult task requires his undivided attention. Still when television comes into the courtroom he must also supervise it. . . . Telecasting is particularly bad where the judge is elected, as is the case in all save a half dozen of our States. The telecasting of the trial becomes a political weapon, which along with other distractions inherent in broadcasting, diverts his attention from the task at hand—the fair trial of the accused. . . .

4. Finally, we cannot ignore the impact of courtroom television on the defendant. Its presence is a form of mental—if not physical—harassment, resembling a police line-up or the third degree. [One] on trial for a specific crime is entitled to his day in court, not in a stadium, or a city or nationwide arena. . . .

It is said that the ever-advancing technique of public communication and the adjustment of the public to its presence may bring about a change in the effect of telecasting upon the fairness of criminal trials. But we are not dealing here with future developments in the field of electronics. Our judgment cannot be rested on the hypothesis of tomorrow but must take the facts as they are presented today.

Chief Justice Burger (joined by Justices Arthur Goldberg and William Douglas) opined:

I wish to emphasize that our condemnation of televised criminal trials is not based on generalities or abstract fears. The record in this case presents a vivid illustration of the inherent prejudice of televised criminal trials and supports our conclusion that this is the appropriate time to make a definitive appraisal of television in the courtroom. . . . I believe that it violates the Sixth Amendment for federal courts and the Fourteenth Amendment for state courts to allow criminal trials to be televised to the public at large. I base this conclusion on three grounds: (1) That the televising of trials diverts the trial from its proper purpose in that it has an inevitable impact on all the trial participants; (2) that it gives the public the wrong impression about the purpose of trials, thereby detracting from the dignity of court proceedings and lessening the reliability of trials; and (3) that it singles out certain defendants and subjects them to trials under prejudicial conditions not experienced by others. . . . The television industry, like other institutions, has a proper area [which] does not extend into an American courtroom. On entering that hallowed sanctuary, where the lives, liberty and property of people are in jeopardy, television representatives have only the rights of the general public, namely, to be present, to observe the proceedings, and thereafter, if they choose, to report them.

The dissent of Justice Stewart (joined by Justices Hugo Black, William Brennan, and Byron White) thought that

the introduction of television into a courtroom is, at least in the present state of the art, an extremely unwise policy. It invites many constitutional risks, and it detracts from the inherent dignity of a courtroom. But I am unable to escalate this personal view into a per se constitutional rule. And I am unable to find, on the specific record of this case, that the circumstances attending the limited televising of the petitioner's trial resulted in the denial of any right guaranteed to him by the United States Constitution. . . . The plain fact of the matter, however, is that none of these [risks or hazards] happened or could have happened in this case. The jurors themselves were prevented from seeing any telecasts of the trial, and completely insulated from association with any members of the public who did see such telecasts. . . .

The suggestions [by members of the majority] that there are limits upon the public's right to know what goes on in the courts causes me deep concern. The idea of imposing upon any medium of communications the burden of justifying its presence is contrary to where I had always thought the presumption must lie in the area of First Amendment freedoms. And the proposition that nonparticipants in a trial might get the "wrong impression" from unfettered reporting and commentary contains an invitation to censorship which I cannot accept.

29. Id. at p. 549.

30. Id. at p. 609.

31. Id. at pp. 542–43.

32. Infra note 23.

33. Infra note 2 at p. 1549.

34. Infra note 24.

35. Id. at pp. 578–79.

36. Id. at p. 581; also infra note 2 at p. 1551.

37. See 84 Mich L Rev 475 (December 1985).

38. See Radio-Television News Directors Association, News Media Coverage of Judicial Proceedings with Cameras and Microphones at B-1 (Jan. 8, 1986).

39. See NLJ (November 30, 1987) at 13 et seq.

40. Id.

41. Chapter 113 (June 15, 1987), Laws of New York, amending Section 218 of the New York Judiciary Law.

Chief Administrative Judge Albert M. Rosenthal on October 9, 1987, announced the text of the proposed rules permitting audiovisual coverage of judicial proceedings on an experimental basis in the state of New York:

Sec. 131.1. Purpose; general provision.

(a) These rules are promulgated to comport with the legislative finding that an enhanced public understanding of the judicial system is important in maintaining a high level of public confidence in the judiciary.

(b) These rules shall be effective for an experimental period from Dec. 1, 1987 through May 31, 1989, and shall apply only in those counties in which audio-visual coverage of judicial proceedings has been authorized by the Chief Administrative Judge of the Courts.

(c) Nothing in these rules is intended to restrict any pre-existing right of the news media to appear at and to report on judicial proceedings in accordance with law.

(d) Nothing in these rules is intended to restrict the power and discretion of the presiding trial judge to control the conduct of judicial proceedings.

(e) No judicial proceedings shall be delayed or continued for the sole purpose of allowing its audio-visual coverage.

(f) Audio-visual coverage shall be conducted without disruption of court activities, without detracting from the dignity or decorum of the court, without compromise of the safety or welfare of persons having business before the court, and without adversely affecting the administration of justice.

Sec. 131.2 Definitions.

For purposes of the part:

(a) "Administrative judge" shall mean the administrative judge of each judicial district; the administrative judge of Nassau County or of Suffolk County; the administrative judge of the Civil Court of the City of New York, the Criminal Court of the City of

New York or the Family Court of the City of New York; or the presiding judge of the Court of Claims. The term ''Chief Administrative Judge also shall mean ''Chief Administrator.''

(b) ''Audio-visual coverage'' or ''coverage'' shall mean the electronic broadcasting or other transmission to the public of radio or television signals from the courtroom, the recording of sound or light in the courtroom for later transmission or reproduction, or the taking of still or motion pictures in the courtroom by the news media.

(c) ''News media'' shall mean any news reporting or news gathering agency and any employee or agent associated with such agency, including television, radio, radio and television networks, news services, newspapers, magazines, trade papers, in-house publications, professional journals, or any other news reporting or news gathering agency, the function of which is to inform the public or some segment thereof.

(d) ''Presiding trial judge'' shall mean the justice or judge presiding over judicial proceedings at which audio-visual coverage is authorized pursuant to this part.

(e) ''Covert or undercover capacity'' shall mean law enforcement activity involving criminal investigation by peace officers or police officers who usually and customarily wear no uniform, badge, or other official identification in public view.

(f) ''Judicial proceedings'' shall mean the proceedings of a court or a judge thereof conducted in a courtroom or any other facility being used as a courtroom.

Sec. 131.3. Application for audio-visual coverage.

(a) Coverage of judicial proceedings shall be permitted only upon order of the presiding trial judge approving an application made by a representative of the news media for permission to conduct such coverage.

(b) An application for permission to conduct coverage of a judicial proceeding shall be made to the presiding trial judge not less than twenty days before the scheduled commencement of that proceeding. Where circumstances require that an applicant cannot apply more than twenty days before the time of proposed coverage, as in the case of an arraignment or under other circumstances that reasonably may preclude such notice, the presiding trial judge may shorten the time period. The application shall be in writing and shall contain proof of service upon all parties to such proceeding. It shall specify such proceeding with sufficient particularity to assist the presiding trial judge in considering the application and shall set forth the nature of the coverage sought, including whether live coverage is sought. The application shall relate to one case or proceeding only.

(c) Where more than one representative of the news media makes an application for coverage of the same judicial proceeding, such applications shall be consolidated and treated as one.

Sec. 131.4. Determination of the application.

(a) Upon receipt of an application pursuant to section 131.3, the presiding trial judge shall conduct such review as may be appropriate, including:

> (1) consultation with counsel to all parties to the proceeding of which coverage is sought, who shall be responsible for identifying any concerns or objections of the parties, prospective witnesses, and victims, if any, with respect to the proposed coverage, and advising the court thereof.
>
> (2) review of all statements or affidavits presented to the presiding trial judge concerning the proposed coverage.

Where the proceedings of which coverage is sought involve a child, a victim, a prospective witness, or a party, any of whom object to such coverage, and in any other appropriate instance, the presiding trial judge may hold such conferences and conduct any direct inquiry as may be fitting.

(b) Consent of the parties, prospective witnesses, victims, or other participants in judicial proceedings of which coverage is sought is not required for approval of an application for such coverage.

(c) In determining an application for coverage, the presiding trial judge shall consider all relevant factors, including but not limited to:

(1) the type of case involved;

(2) whether the coverage would cause psychological or physical harm to any participant;

(3) whether the coverage would interfere with the fair administration of justice, the advancement of a fair trial, or the rights of the parties;

(4) whether the coverage would interfere with any law enforcement activity;

(5) whether the proceedings would involve lewd or scandalous matters;

(6) the objectionss of any of the parties, prospective witnesses, victims, or other participants in the proceedings of which coverage is sought;

(7) the physical structure of the courtroom and the likelihood that any equipment required to conduct coverage of proceedings can be installed and operated without disturbance to those proceedings or any other proceedings in the courthouse; and

(8) the extent to which the coverage would be barred by law in the judicial proceeding of which coverage is sought.

The presiding trial judge also shall consider and give great weight to the fact that any party, prospective witness, victim, or other participant in the proceeding is a child.

(d) Following review of an application for coverage of a judicial proceeding, the presiding trial judge shall issue an order, in writing, approving such application, in whole or in part, or denying it. Such order shall state the basis for its determination and shall be included in the record of such proceedings.

(e) Before denying an application for coverage, the presiding trial judge shall consider whether such coverage properly could be approved with the imposition of special limitations, including but not limited to:

(1) delayed broadcast of the proceedings subject to coverage;

(2) prohibition of audio-visual coverage of individual parties, witnesses, or other trial participants, or portions of the proceedings; or

(3) prohibition of video coverage of individual parties, witnesses, or other trial participants, or portions of the proceedings.

Sec. 131.5 Review

(a) Any order determining an application for permission to provide coverage, rendered pursuant to subdivision (d) of section 131.4 of this part, shall be subject to review by the administrative judge in such form, including telephone conference, as he or she may determine, upon the request of a person who is aggrieved thereby and who is either:

(1) a news media applicant; or

(2) a party, victim, or prospective witness who objected to coverage.

(b) Upon review of a presiding trial judge's order determining an application for permission to provide coverage, the administrative judge shall uphold such order unless it is found that the order reflects an abuse of discretion by the presiding trial judge, in which event the administrative judge may direct such modification of the presiding trial judge's order as may be deemed appropriate. Any order directing a modification or overruling a presiding trial judge's order determining an application for coverage shall be in writing.

(c) No judicial proceeding shall be delayed or continued to allow for review by an administrative judge of an order denying coverage in whole or in part.

(d) This section shall authorize review by the administrative judge only of a presiding trial judge's order pursuant to paragraph (c) of subdivision three of section 218 of the Judiciary Law determining an application for permission to provide coverage of judicial proceedings and shall not authorize review of any other orders or decisions of the presiding trial judge relating to such coverage.

Sec. 131.6. Mandatory pretrial conference.

(a) Where a presiding trial judge has approved, in whole or in part, an application for coverage of any judicial proceeding, the judge, before any such coverage is to begin, shall conduct a pretrial conference for the purpose of reviewing, with counsel and with representatives of the news media who will provide such coverage, any objections to coverage that have been raised, the scope of coverage to be permitted, the nature and extent of the technical equipment and personnel to be deployed, and the restrictions on coverage to be observed. The court may include in the conference any other person whom it deems appropriate, including prospective witnesses and their representatives.

(b) Where two or more representatives of the news media are parties to an approved application for coverage, no such coverage may begin until all such representatives have agreed upon a pooling arrangement for their respective news media prior to the pretrial conference. Such pooling arrangement shall include the designation of a pool operator for the electronic and motion picture media and a pool operator for the still photography media, as appropriate. It also shall include procedures for the cost sharing and dissemination of audio-visual material and shall make due provision for educational users' needs for full coverage of entire proceedings. The presiding trial judge shall not be called upon to mediate or resolve any dispute as to such arrangement.

(c) In determining the scope of coverage to be permitted, the presiding trial judge shall be guided by a consideration of all relevant factors, including those prescribed in subdivision (c) of section 131.4 of this part. Wherever necessary or appropriate, the presiding trial judge shall, at any time before or during the proceeding, proscribe, modify, expand, or impose special limitations on coverage, such as those prescribed in subdivision (e) of section 131.4.

Sec. 131.7. Use and deployment of equipment and personnel by the news media.

(a) Equipment and personnel.

(1) No more than two electronic or motion picture cameras and two camera operators shall be permitted in any proceeding.

(2) No more than one photographer to operate two still cameras, with not more than two lenses for each camera, shall be permitted in any proceeding.

(3) No more than one audio system for broadcast purposes shall be permitted in any proceeding. Audio pickup for all news media purposes shall be effectuated through existing audio systems in the court facility. If no technically suitable audio system is available, microphones and related wiring essential for me-

dia purposes shall be supplied by those persons providing coverage. Any microphones and sound wiring shall be unobtrusive and placed where designated by the presiding trial judge.

(4) Notwithstanding the provisions of paragraph one, two, and three of this subdivision, the presiding trial judge on a finding of special circumstances may modify any restriction on the amount of equipment or number of operating personnel in the courtroom, compatible with the dignity of the court of the judicial process.

(b) Sound and light criteria.

(1) Only electronic and motion picture cameras, audio equipment, and still camera equipment that do not produce distracting sound or light may be employed to cover judicial proceedings. The equipment designated . . . shall be deemed acceptable.

(2) Use of equipment other than that authorized . . . may be permitted by the presiding trial judge provided the judge is satisfied that the equipment sought to be utilized meets the sound and light criteria specified in paragraph one of this subdivision. A failure to obtain advance approval shall preclude use of such equipment in the coverage of the judicial proceeding.

(3) No motorized drives, moving lights, flash attachments, or sudden lighting changes shall be permitted during coverage of judicial proceedings.

(4) No light or signal visible or audible to trial participants shall be used on any equipment during coverage to indicate whether it is operating.

(5) With the concurrence of the presiding trial judge and the administrative judge, modifications and additions may be made in light sources existing in the court facility, provided such modifications or additions are installed and maintained at media expense and are not distracting or otherwise offensive.

(c) Location of equipment and personnel. Electronic and motion picture cameras, still cameras, and camera personnel shall be positioned in such locations as shall be designated by the presiding trial judge. The areas designated shall provide the news media with reasonable access to the persons they wish to cover while causing the least possible interference with court proceedings. Equipment that is not necessary for audio-visual coverage from inside the courtroom shall be located in an area outside the courtroom.

(d) Movement of equipment and media personnel. During the proceedings, operating personnel shall not move about, nor shall there be placement, movement or removal of equipment, or the changing of film, film magazines or lenses. All such activities shall take place each day before the proceeding begins, after it ends, or during a recess.

(e) Identifying insignia. Identifying marks, call letters, words, and symbols shall be concealed on all equipment. Persons operating such equipment shall not display any identifying insignia on their clothing.

(f) The presiding trial judge may impose any other restrictions on the use and deployment of equipment and personnel as may be appropriate.

Sec. 131.8. Additional restrictions on coverage.

(a) No audio pickup or audio broadcast of conferences that occur in a court facility between attorneys and their clients, between co-counsel of a client, or between counsel and the presiding trial judge, shall be permitted without the prior express consent of all participants in the conference.

(b) No conference in chambers shall be subject to coverage.

(c) No coverage of the selection of the prospective jury during voir dire shall be permitted.

(d) No coverage of the jury, or of any juror or alternate juror, while in the jury box, in the courtroom, in the jury deliberation room, or during recess, or while going to or from the deliberation room at any time, shall be permitted.

(e) No coverage shall be permitted of a witness, who as a peace officer or police officer acted in a covert or undercover capacity in connection with the proceedings being covered, without the prior written consent of such witness.

(f) No coverage shall be permitted of a witness, who as a peace officer or police officer is currently engaged in a covert or undercover capacity, without the prior written consent of such witness.

(g) No coverage shall be permitted of the victim in a prosecution for rape, sodomy, sexual abuse, or other sex offense under article one hundred thirty or section 255.25 of the Penal Law.

(h) No coverage of any participant shall be permitted if the presiding trial judge finds that such coverage is liable to endanger the safety of any person.

(i) No coverage of any judicial proceedings that are by law closed to the public, or that may be closed to the public and that have been closed by the presiding trial judge, shall be permitted.

The restrictions specified in subdivisions (a) through (i) may not be waived or modified except as provided therein.

Sec. 131.9. Supervision of audio-visual coverage.

(a) Coverage of judicial proceedings shall be subject to the continuing supervision of the presiding trial judge. No coverage shall take place within the courtroom during recesses or at any time when the presiding trial judge is not present and presiding.

(b) Notwithstanding the approval of an application for permission to provide coverage of judicial proceedings, the presiding trial judge shall have discretion throughout such proceedings to revoke such approval or to limit the coverage authorized in any way. In the exercise of this discretion, the presiding trial judge shall be especially sensitive and responsive to the needs and concerns of all parties, victims, witnesses, and other participants in such proceedings, particularly where the proceedings inappropriately threaten the privacy or sensibilities of victims, or where they involve children or sex offenses or other matters that may be lewd or scandalous. The presiding trial judge shall be under a continuing obligation to order the discontinuation or modification of coverage where necessary to shield the identity or otherwise insure the protection of any such person, party, witness, or victim, or in order to preserve the welfare of a child.

Sec. 131.10. Reports.

(a) Immediately upon the conclusion of any judicial proceedings in a trial court where coverage was conducted, the presiding trial judge and counsel for all parties shall each prepare and file a report in a form prescribed by the Chief Administrative Judge of the Courts, assessing the effect of the coverage upon the proceedings. The presiding trial judge also shall invite all parties, witnesses, victims, and other participants in the proceedings covered to prepare and file like reports. All reports shall set forth the writer's general reaction to the coverage, together with any recommendations for change in the procedures that were followed. Reports shall be filed with the Chief Administrative Judge and shall be available for public inspection and copying at the Office of Public Information, Office of Court Administration, 270 Broadway, New York 10007.

(b) In preparing the report as required by paragraph (a), the presiding trial judge shall ask the foreman of the jury, if the proceedings covered included a jury trial, for the jury's reaction to the coverage, and such reaction shall be included in the judge's report.

(c) Until May 31, 1989, and unless the Chief Administrative Judge shall otherwise provide, news media participating in coverage of judicial proceedings shall, for purposes of evaluating this experimental project, transmit to the Office of Court Administration copies of any audio-visual material aired, within five business days after such airing.

(d) The Chief Administrative Judge shall develop criteria as a basis for the report to be filed by the Chief Administrative Judge pursuant to law.

Sec. 131.11. Appellate courts.

These rules shall not apply to coverage of proceedings in appellate courts or affect the rules governing such coverage contained in Part 29 of the Rules of the Chief Judge (22 NYCRR Part 29).

Judge Rosenthal is authorized under the New York legislation to select the counties in which the telecommunications equipment will be allowed. Under the rules, news organizations must make a written request to cover a proceeding at least twenty days in advance of the proceeding, but judges are given discretion to shorten that period of time due to impracticality. Pooling arrangements must also be worked out by the media so that the maximum equipment allowed in a courtroom at any one time would be no more than two electronic and two motion picture cameras, two still cameras of only one photographer, and one audio system.

42. Id. Also note NYLJ (July 2, 1987) at pp. 1 et seq.

43. Sec. 218(6)(a)(ii) of the New York Judiciary Law.

44. Sec. 218(3)(d).

45. Sec. 218(3)(b).

46. Sec. 218(3)(c).

47. Sec. 218(7)(d).

48. Sec. 218(7)(c).

49. Sec. 218(7)(e), (f).

50. See New York Times (November 25, 1987) at B3; also see NYLJ (December 1, 1987) at 1 et seq., where the trial judge is quoted to the effect that

the development of the evidence by the defendants should be in the same setting as was the development of the evidence by the prosecutor. . . . The court has never deprived the media access to any of the proceedings in this case. . . . The Court's concern about cameras triggering demonstrations or confrontations in the courtroom is not speculative but real, and it is based on the Court's observations throughout two and one half months of trial.

51. See New York Times (December 5, 1987) at 30.

52. See New York Times (December 8, 1987) at B5.

53. See NYLJ (January 22, 1988) at 1 et seq.
54. New York Supreme Court, Bronx County, decided January 24, 1988.
55. According to the court,

the news media applicants stated that they had worked out a pool arrangement and requested that the still photographers be permitted to rotate into the courtroom for five minute periods. They also stated that the cameras would be 35 mm, using black and white film, and would utilize existing light sources, i.e., there would be no flash required. It was also requested, if permission were granted, that the photographs be permitted to be taken from the empty jury box.

I then reviewed all the relevant factors, set forth in section 131.4(c), and determined that: (1) this case, involving a charge of quadruple homicide, was not one that should not receive coverage; (2) the coverage of the scheduled hearing would not cause harm to any participant; (3) the coverage would not interfere with the fair administration of justice, a fair trial, or the rights of the parties; (4) the coverage would not interfere with any law enforcement activity; (5) the proceedings do not involve lewd or scandalous matters; (6) there have been no objections from any of the parties or from counsel for the Department of Corrections concerning the prospective witnesses for the department, indeed, all counsel have expressly stated there were no objections; (7) the physical structure of the courtroom (Room 415, Bronx Supreme Court) is such that the requested coverage will not disturb the proceedings; and (8) there is no other legal impediment to the coverage. Accordingly, the applications for coverage through the use of still photography, is approved subject to the following:

(1) Only one photographer at a time will be permitted, with two still cameras and not more than two lens for each camera.

(2) Each photographer may rotate, under the supervision of uniformed court officers for periods of five minutes.

(3) Each photographer may photograph from the empty jury box.

(4) No motorized drives or flash attachments shall be permitted.

(5) No conference in chambers shall be subject to coverage.

(6) No coverage shall take place within the courtroom; whether during recesses, or at any other time, when I am not present and actually presiding. The approved coverage of this proceeding shall be subject to my continuing supervision.

(7) I retain the discretion throughout the proceedings to revoke my approval of coverage and to limit the coverage authorized in any way.

(8) Immediately upon the conclusion of the proceedings, counsel for all parties shall each prepare and file a report, in a form prescribed by the Chief Administrative Judge of the Courts, assessing the effect of the coverage upon the proceeding. All parties, witnesses, and any other participants in the proceedings covered including any representative of the news media present during such coverage, are also invited to prepare and file like reports. All reports shall set forth the writer's general reaction to the coverage, together with any recommendations for change in the procedures that were followed. Reports shall be filed with the Chief Administrative Judge and shall be available for public inspection and copying at the Office of Communications, Office of Court Administration, Room 1008, 270 Broadway, New York, New York 10007.

56. Vol. 48 at pp. 511 et seq.
57. 695 F2d 1278 (11th Cir., 1983), cert den 461 US 931 (1983).

58. See United States v. Kerley, 753 F2d 617 (7th Cir., 1985) to the same effect.

59. Infra note 58.

60. 24 NY2d 395, 248 NE2d 588 (1969), cert den 396 US 886 (1969).

61. 123 Ariz 243, 599 P2d 199 (1979).

62. 413 A2d 58 (R.I., 1980).

63. Infra note 44 at pp. 488 et seq. Also infra note 22.

64. See Cox Broadcasting Corp. v. Cohn, 420 US 469 (1975) at p. 496.

65. See United States ex rel Lloyd v. Vincent, 520 F2d 1272 (2d Cir., 1975), cert den 423 US 937 (1975).

66. See United States ex rel Smallwood v. LaValle, 373 F Supp 1148 (EDNY, 1974), cert den 421 US 920 (1975).

67. See United States v. Geise, 158 F Supp 821 (Alas., 1958), cert den 361 US 842 (1959).

68. 381 US 479 (1965).

69. See generally sec. 652A-652E of Restatement (Second) of Torts (1976).

70. See, for example, Landmark Communications, Inc. v. Virginia, 435 US 829 (1978) and Smith v. Daily Mail Publishing Co., 443 US 97 (1979).

71. See Davis v. Alaska, 415 US 308 (1974) and Chambers v. Mississippi, 410 US 284 (1973).

72. Infra note 2 at p. 1554.

73. See United States v. Valenzuela-Bernal, 458 US 858 (1982) at p. 867.

APPENDIX: PROPOSED MODEL GUIDELINES*

Subject at all times to the authority of the Judge to

(i) control the conduct of proceedings before the Court;

(ii) ensure decorum and prevent distractions; and

(iii) ensure the fair administration of justice in pending case, electronic media and still photography coverage of public judicial proceedings in the Courts of this state may be allowed in accordance with standards of conduct and technology adopted by the Supreme Court of ________.

(I) Definitions

"Judicial proceedings" or "proceedings" as referred to in these rules shall include all public trials, hearings or other proceedings in a trial or appellate

*From "Cameras in the Courtroom: Guidelines for State Criminal Trials," 84 Mich. L. Rev. pp. 475–516 (Dec. 1985). Reprinted with permission from the *Michigan Law Review*.

court, for which expanded media coverage is requested, except those specifically excluded by these rules.

"Expanded media coverage" includes broadcasting, televising, electronic recording or photographing of judicial proceedings for the purpose of gathering and disseminating news to the public.

"Judge" means the magistrate, district associate judge, or district judge presiding in a trial court proceeding or the presiding judge or justice in an appellate proceeding.

(II) Standards for Authorizing Coverage

(a) The judge has discretion to allow or deny expanded media coverage. In making that decision, the judge should consider the following factors:

1. whether there is a reasonable likelihood that expanded media coverage would interfere with the rights of the parties to a fair trial; or
2. whether there is a reasonable likelihood that expanded media coverage would unduly detract from the solemnity, decorum and dignity of the court.[211]

(b) There shall be no expanded media coverage of any court proceeding which, under the laws of the state of ______________, are required to be held in private. Additionally, no such coverage shall be permitted in any cases involving sex crimes, juvenile proceedings, marriage dissolution, adoption, child custody, motions to suppress evidence, police informants, undercover agents, and trade secrets, unless consent on the record is obtained from all parties (including the parent or guardian of a minor child).[212]

(III) Liaison

The Administrative Director of the Courts shall maintain communication and liaison with media representatives so as to insure smooth working relationships.[213]

(IV) Limitations on Expanded Coverage

(a) Notwithstanding an authorization to conduct expanded media coverage of a proceeding, there shall be no expanded media coverage of

1. communications between counsel and client or co-counsel;
2. bench conferences;

3. *in camera* hearings;
4. communications between judges in appellate proceedings;
5. members of the jury at any time, including voir dire;[214]
6. hearings that take place outside the presence of the jury

(b) No witness who expresses to the judge any prior objection shall be photographed by any camera, nor shall the testimony of such a witness be broadcast or telecast.[215]

(c) There shall be no expanded media coverage within the courtroom during the recesses or at any other time in which the trial judge is not present and presiding.

(V) Authority to Impose Restrictions on Expanded Media Coverage

In authorizing expanded media coverage, a judge may impose such restrictions or limitations as may be necessary to preserve the dignity of the court and to protect the parties, witnesses, and jurors. A judge may terminate expanded media coverage at any time upon a finding that

1. rules established herein or additional rules imposed by the judge have been violated; or

2. substantial rights of individual participants or rights to a fair trial will be prejudiced by such coverage if it is allowed to continue.[216]

(VI) Procedure

(a) *Prior request for permission and notice.* Requests for permission for expanded media coverage in the courtroom shall be made in writing at least ten days before the proceedings are scheduled to begin, unless such time is reduced or extended by court order upon a showing of good cause. The attorneys of record shall be notified by the Court Administrator or by the Clerk of the Court at least seven days in advance of the time the proceedings are scheduled to begin unless such time is reduced or extended by court order. The written permission of the judge shall be made a part of the record of the proceedings.[217]

(b) *Objections.* A party to a proceeding objecting to expanded media coverage shall file a written objection, stating the grounds therefore, at least three days before commencement of the proceeding. All witnesses shall be advised by counsel proposing to introduce their testimony of their right to object to expanded media coverage of their testimony and all objections shall be filed prior to commencement of the proceeding.

All objections shall be heard and determined by the judge prior to commencement of the proceedings. Time for filing of objections may be extended or reduced at the discretion of the judge. A criminal defendant shall be entitled to an immediate appeal of a decision to permit televising.[218]

(VII) Limitations on Broadcasting

(a) Film, videotape, photography and audio reproductions may not be used for advertising purposes.

(b) Television broadcasters must present balanced coverage of the prosecution and the defense.

(c) None of the film, videotape, still photographs or audio reproductions developed during, or by virtue of, coverage of a judicial proceeding shall be admissible as evidence in the proceeding out of which it arose, any proceeding subsequent or collateral thereto, or upon any retrial or appeal of such proceedings.[219]

(VIII) Media Personnel

Media representatives shall conduct themselves in a manner consistent with the decorum and dignity of the courtroom. The following practices shall be observed in this regard:

(a) Media representatives shall present a neat appearance in keeping with the dignity of the proceedings.

(b) Personnel shall not wear clothing bearing any insignia or identification of the individual or network involved. Identifying marks, call letters, logos, symbols and legends shall be concealed on all equipment.

(c) Media representatives shall not move about the court facility while proceedings are in session.[220]

Comment:
If the judge believes that the appearance and position of media personnel in the courtroom might mislead the jury into thinking that the media personnel are officers of the court, the judge should instruct the jury that they are not associated with the court in any official manner.

(IX) Equipment

Expanded media coverage shall be conducted only under the following conditions:

(a) *Equipment specifications*. Equipment must be unobtrusive and must not produce distracting sounds. In addition, such equipment must satisfy the following criteria:

1. *Television cameras and related equipment.*

    (a) Not more than one portable television camera [film camera—16 mm sound on film (self blimped) or video-tape electronic camera], operated by not more than one person, shall be permitted in any trial court proceeding.

    (b) Television cameras are to be designed or modified so that participants in the judicial proceeding are unable to determine when recording is occurring.

    (c) Where possible, recording and broadcasting equipment that is not a component part of a television camera shall be located outside of the courtroom.

    (d) The camera operators shall remain in a single location throughout the proceeding.

    (e) No artificial lighting device of any kind shall be employed in connection with the television camera.

2. *Audio*. The court's audio system shall be used if technically feasible and, in that event, the media will ensure that they do not interfere with the court's use of the system. If the court's system is not technically suitable, then all audio recording shall be done on one audio system installed by the media at their own expense. All microphones and related wiring shall be unobtrusive and shall not interfere with the movement of those in the courtroom. Microphones for use of counsel and judges shall be equipped with on/off switches. Where possible, electronic audio recording equipment and any operating personnel shall be located outside of the courtroom.

3. *Still Cameras*. All photographs shall be taken by one still photographer using an unobtrusive tripod and using not more than two still cameras. The photographer shall remain in a single location throughout the proceeding. Such still camera equipment shall produce no greater sound or light than a 35 mm Leica "M" Series Rangefinder camera, and no artificial lighting device of any kind shall be employed in connection with a still camera.

4. *Lighting*. No movie lights, flash attachments, or sudden lighting changes

shall be permitted during a proceeding. No modification or addition of lighting equipment shall be permitted without the permission of the judge.

5. *Operating Signals.* No visible or audible light or signal (tally light) shall be used on any equipment.

6. In proceedings involving a jury, all equipment and personnel must be present during the entirety of the proceeding.

7. It shall be the affirmative duty of media personnel to demonstrate to the judge adequately in advance of any proceeding that the equipment sought to be utilized meets the sound and light criteria described herein. A failure to obtain advance judicial approval for equipment shall preclude its use in any proceeding.

8. All equipment shall be in place and tested fifteen minutes in advance of the time the court is called to order and shall be placed in an unobtrusive or hidden location designated by the judge.

9. Equipment involved in expanded media coverage shall not be placed in, or removed from, the courtroom except prior to commencement or after adjournment of proceedings each day, or during a recess. Neither television film, magazines, video cassettes, nor still camera film or lenses shall be changed within a courtroom except during a recess in the proceedings.[221]

(b) *Pooling arrangements.* The media shall be solely responsible for designating one media representative to conduct each of the categories of expanded media coverage listed in subsection (1) of this section, and for arranging an open and impartial distribution scheme with a distribution point located outside the courtroom. If no agreement can be reached on either of these matters, then there shall be no expanded media coverage. Neither judges nor other court personnel shall be called upon to resolve any disputes that may arise in this connection.[222]

(X) Agreement of Media Representatives

All persons who request and are granted permission to cover a judicial proceeding are subject to this plan and agree to abide by its provisions.[223]

NOTES

211. For similar state provisions, see e.g., Alaska Code of Judicial Conduct Canon 3A(7)(a) in Alaska Rules of Court (1985); Ariz. Code of Judicial Conduct Canon 3A(7)(b) in Ariz. Rules of Court (1985); Colo. Code of Ju-

dicial Conduct Canon 3A(8)(b) in Colo. Court Rules (1984) (temporary); Ohio Code of Judicial Conduct Canon 3A(7)(c)(ii) in Ohio Rules of Court (1986); Okla. Code of Judicial Conduct Canon 3A(7)(b) in Okla. Court Rules and Procedure (1985-86); Tenn. Code of Judicial Conduct Canon 3A(7)(c) in Tenn. Rules of Court (1985).

212. See notes 138-56 supra and accompanying text. For similar state provisions, see, for example, In re Arkansas Bar Assn., 271 Ark. 358, 362-65, 609 S.W.2d 28, 30-31 (1980), modified, In re Modification of Code of Judicial Conduct Relating to Broadcasting & Photographing Court Proceedings, 275 Ark. 495, 628 S.W.2d 573 (1982); Conn. Code of Judicial Conduct Canon 3A(7A)(4) in Conn. Rules of Court (1986); Iowa Code of Judicial Conduct Canon 3A(7)2(d) in Iowa Rules of Court (1985); N.C. Code of Judicial Conduct Canon 3A(7)(2)(b & c) in N.C. Rules of Court (1985) (temporary).

213. See, e.g., Hawaii Code of Judicial Conduct 19.1(e) in Rules of Court: The Judiciary of Hawaii (1983); Iowa Code of Judicial Conduct Canon 3A(7)3(a) in Iowa Rules of Court (1985); Tenn. Code of Judicial Conduct Canon 3A(7), Media Guidelines 3 & 4 in Tenn. Rules of Court (1985).

214. See, e.g., Conn. Code of Judicial Conduct 3A(7A)(6 & 7), in Conn. Rules of Court (1986); Hawaii Code of Judicial Conduct 19.1(g)(2 & 3), in Rules of Court: The Judiciary of Hawaii (1983); Iowa Code of Judicial Conduct Canon 3A(7)2(e & f) in Iowa Rules of Court (1985); In re Canon 3A(7), 9 Media L. Rptr. 1778, 1779 (Minn. 1984); see also notes 125-37 supra and accompanying text.

215. See, e.g., Ga. Code of Judicial Conduct Canon 3A(7)(c)(ii), in Ga. Court Rules and Procedure (1986); Kan. Rules Relating to Judicial Conduct Canon 3A(7)(c)(ii) in Kan. Court Rules and Procedure (1986); Md. Court Rules and Judicial Canons Rule 1209(e)(i)(1984); In re Canon 3A(7), 9 Media L. Rptr. 1778, 1779 (Minn. 1984); Ohio Code of Judicial Conduct Canon 3A(7)(c)(iii) in Ohio Rules of Court (1986); Okla. Code of Judicial Conduct Canon 3A(7)(c) in Okla. Court of Rules and Procedure (1985-86).

216. See, e.g., Colo. Code of Judicial Conduct Canon 3A(8)(b) in Colo. Court Rules (1984); Iowa Code of Judicial Conduct Canon 3A(7)2(h) in Iowa Rules of Court (1985).

217. See, e.g., Iowa Code of Judicial Conduct Canon 3A(7)3(b) in Iowa Rules of Court (1985); see also notes 157-60 supra and accompanying text.

218. See Iowa Code of Judicial Conduct Canon 3A(7)3(c) in Iowa Rules of Court (1985); see also notes 161-72 supra and accompanying text.

219. See, e.g., In re Canon 3A(7), 9 Media L. Rptr. 1778, 1781 (Minn. 1984); see also notes 173-85 supra and accompanying text.

220. See, e.g., Cal. Civ. & Crim. Ct. R. 980(b)(3) (West 1979); Colo. Code of Judicial Conduct Canon 3A(8)(e)(III) in Colo. Court Rules (1984); Iowa Code of Judicial Conduct Canon 3A(7)4(e & f) in Iowa Rules of Court

(1985); Md. Court Rules and Judicial Canons Rules 1209(f)(10)(1984); In re Canon 3A(7), 9 Media L. Rptr. 1778, 1780 (Minn. 1984); Pa. Code of Judicial Conduct Canon 3A(7)(c)(i) in Pa. Rules of Court (1986).

[Notes 221 and 222 have been omitted for lack of space.]

223. See In re Canon 3A(7), 5 Media L. Rep. 2494, 2496 (Alaska 1979).

6

The Right to Gather Information versus the Right to Disseminate Information

The press and media under the First Amendment are accorded the right of access to the criminal courtroom,[1] but within that context there are innumerable situations where courts have encountered difficulty with given fact patterns. A recent example occurred in Associated Press v. Bell,[2] where the press and media sought to view a videotape confession of Robert Chambers who allegedly killed a young woman in Central Park in New York City. At the "suppression hearing," attorneys for the accused contended that disclosure of the content of the confession could prejudice potential jurors and thus deny the accused his right to a fair trial under the Sixth Amendment.[3] But the New York Court of Appeals was unwilling to evoke closure and bar the press and media from its right to gather news: "By denying public access to the suppression hearings on a 'possibility' that there might be tainted, non-public evidence that might impair the selection of an impartial jury, which could very likely be said of every suppression hearing in every publicized case, the trial court improperly closed the door on [the news media's] First Amendment rights." The highest New York court continued: "It is apparent that a hypothetical risk of prejudice or taint cannot justify categorical denial of public access to suppression hearings because, as a general matter, the important interests of both the accused and the public can be accommodated." Prejudiced jurors can be identified through a careful voir dire, according to the court. But the right of access is not absolute, for the burden is on the defendant to prove that his right to a fair trial may be compromised by coverage of a suppression hearing. The court concluded: "There was no specific finding of a substantial probability that the defendant's right to a fair trial would be prejudiced by publicity that closure would prevent, and no finding that reasonable alternatives to closure could not adequately protect defendant's fair trial rights."[4]

On the other hand, the Florida Supreme Court on February 19, 1987, denied the press and media access to unfiled pre-trial discovery depositions in Palm Beach Newspapers, Inc. v. Burk.[5] The ruling was based on the determination that the taking of depositions in a criminal case was not a judicial proceeding until such time as the depositions were transcribed and filed with the court.

In United States v. Salerno,[6] the federal district court for the Southern District of New York was asked by a television network to permit a copy of a videotaped deposition of an imprisoned former labor leader that was used in an ongoing trial to be shown on television. About two weeks previous, on June 1 and 2, 1987, the jury was shown the videotaped deposition in a courtroom open to the press and the public. The court turned down the request of CBS, Inc. on the ground that the public's common law right to access to judicial records did not require the release for television of the deposition in question. The witness's "privacy concerns are sufficiently extraordinary to restrict access in this case. . . . [furthermore] he is not on trial in the Salerno case. The deposition video-tape is not itself evidence of any crime. . . . We see no reason to subject a witness to local or national television exposure simply because he was too sick to fly to New York and the government chose to make its case on video-tape. The deposition room in Missouri [where the deposition was taken] was simply an extension of the Southern District courtroom."[7] However, on September 15, 1987, the Second U.S. Court of Appeals in United States v. Esposito and Biaggi[8] expanded the public's right to obtain secret pre-trial documents in criminal cases when the federal appellate court overturned the district court's ruling that withheld some key documents from the press and media. The access right of press and media was held to extend to motion papers and even wiretap material, based on "a qualified First Amendment right of access [which] extends to such documents. . . . The Supreme Court has indicated that a qualified First Amendment right of access to criminal proceedings extends to certain pre-trial proceedings."[9] Documents need not be automatically disclosed to press and media but may be withheld only if specific findings are made on the record to show that a "narrowly tailored" sealing was essential.

The right to gather information and the right to disseminate information, it is argued, are part and parcel of the greater right to know, protected under the First Amendment.[10] Professor Thomas Emerson expressed this view in his "Legal Foundations of the Right to Know":

> The right to know fits into the First Amendment and whole system of freedom of expression. Reduced to its simplest terms the concept includes two closely related features: First, the right to read, to listen, to see, and to otherwise receive communications; and second, the right to obtain information as a basis for transmitting ideas or facts to others. Together these constitute the reverse side of the coin from the right to communicate. But the coin is one piece, namely the system of freedom of expression.[11]

In 1972 the U.S. Supreme Court first expressly recognized the right to gather information as having constitutional dimensions. The issue in Branzburg v. Hayes[12] was whether news reporters could be required to reveal their news sources to grand juries. The 5-4 vote of the Court held that news reporters could be compelled to disclose where such testimony is necessary to promote the compelling state interest in ensuring effective grand jury proceedings. However, the compelled testimony was not deemed by the majority of the Court to have entirely impaired the press's and media's right to gather news: "Without some protection for seeking out the news," however, "freedom of the press could be eviscerated."[13] It would appear that this right to gather news or information was the logical and necessary antecedent of the right to disseminate news or information. Justice Stewart in his dissent opined: "There is a right to publish without prior governmental approval, a right to distribute information, and a right to receive printed matter. No less important to the news dissemination process is the gathering of information. News must not be unnecessarily cut off at its source, for without freedom to acquire information the right to publish would be impermissibly compromised. Accordingly, a right to gather news, of some dimensions, must exist."

Criminal trials constitute a source of information, according to Chief Justice Burger in his 1980 opinion in Richmond Newspapers, Inc v. Virginia[14] that is particularly amenable to the constitutional right of access.[15] Criminal trials are under governmental rather than private control; criminal trials have historically been open to the public; free accessibility to criminal trials helps promote the fair and proper administration of justice; and criminal trials represent a part of government of particular concern to the citizenry: "It would be difficult to single out any aspect of government of higher concern and importance to the people than the manner in which criminal trials are conducted."[16] The chief justice then opined: "What this means in the context of trials is that the First Amendment guarantees of speech and press, standing alone, prohibit government from summarily closing courtroom doors which had long been open to the public at the time that [First] Amendment was adopted."[17] The right to gather news or information is enhanced, according to the chief justice, by recognition of the role played by the "print and electronic media" as "surrogates for the public": "While media representatives enjoy the same right of access as the public, they often are provided special seating and priority of entry so that they may report what people in attendance have seen and heard. This 'contributes to public understanding of the rule of law and to comprehension of the functioning of the entire criminal justice system.' "[18] But the press and media are not entitled to special exemption from the general rules of search warrants, as illustrated by Zurcher v. Stanford Daily.[19] Here the highest Court refused to give the press and media special immunity from search warrants issued by a judicial magistrate upon a showing of probable cause to believe that the files of a student newspaper contained pictures that would be useful evidence in identifying the leaders of a riotous demonstration that resulted in felonious assaults upon police officers.[20]

The presence of cameras in the criminal courtroom is obviously essential to the right to gather news or information, but several states have totally banned cameras or have mandated their exclusion from the proceeding upon the objection of a single participant, for whatever reason.[21] The defendant's right to a fair trial under the Sixth Amendment is apparently protected by this functional ban on cameras; but the ban is oblivious to the demands of First Amendment policies on the right of the press and media to gather news or information.[22] Even where the defendant requests cameras in the criminal courtroom, the federal courts still ban the intrusion, as illustrated in United States v. Kerley.[23]

A variation on this theme is seen in Oklahoma where a prospective witness may rightfully object to camera coverage for his or her testimony, though the rest of the criminal trial is subject to camera coverage.[24] A third variation is to give the trial judge the discretion to allow or disallow camera coverage of the criminal trial, as in Arizona, California, and Florida. In Arizona the trial judge must initially determine whether camera coverage "would have a substantially greater adverse impact upon the witness or his testimony than non-electronic and non-photographic coverage would have."[25] California simply admonishes the trial judge to limit coverage "in the interests of justice to protect the rights of the parties."[26] And in Florida the trial judge may permit but is not required to exclude electronic media coverage, unless such coverage would have "a substantial effect upon the particular individual which would be qualitatively different from the effect on members of the public in general."[27] The U.S. Supreme Court in Chandler v. Florida[28] had, in 1981, nevertheless given the accused defendant relief from press and media coverage if he could prove that the coverage either "compromised the ability of the jury to judge him fairly" or "had an adverse impact on the trial participants sufficient to constitute a denial of due process."[29] But this two-prong test may not take into account the prejudicial subtleties that television coverage, for example, imposes on the trial participants whose demeanor, cogency of argument, and even willingness to speak freely may be adversely affected by the press and media coverage.[30]

The right of the press and media to gather news or information does not encompass a right of access to all sources of news and information within governmental control, as illustrated by Houchins v. KQED, Inc.,[31] which barred access of press and media to a penal institution where they sought to conduct interviews with prison inmates and to use audiovisual equipment inside the jail. Chief Justice Burger pointed out that the First Amendment mandates neither a right of access to government-controlled sources of information nor a special access right for the institutional media. The dissent of Justice Stevens recalled, "Our system of self-government assumes the existence of an informed citizenry. . . . Without some protection for the acquisition of information about the operation of public institutions such as prisons by the public at large, the process of self-governance contemplated by the Framers would be stripped of its substance."[32] But the press and media have no greater right of access to prisons, for example, than members of the general public.[33] Yet "a responsible press has always been regarded as the handmaiden of effective judicial administration, especially in the criminal field.''[34]

The other side of the coin (one side being the right to gather information or news) is the right of the press and media to disseminate information or news. But first the right of the public to ''receive'' news or information about criminal trials must be recognized. Justice Douglas in his dissent in Branzburg v. Hayes[35] observed, ''Effective self-government cannot succeed unless the people are immersed in a steady, robust, unimpeded, and uncensored flow of opinion and reporting.''[36] The right of the public to ''receive information and ideas'' is protected by the First Amendment. In Martin v. Struthers,[37] the highest Court solemnized that ''this freedom embraces the right to distribute literature and necessarily protects the right to receive it.''[38]

The transcript of the criminal trial and in particular the transcript of the trial judge's charge to the jury were the objectives of a suit by a newspaper in the late 1950s in New York Post Corporation v. Leibowitz.[39] After the acquittal of a probationary police officer charged with the crime of manslaughter in the first degree, arising out of the fatal shooting of a fifteen-year-old boy, the newspaper requested a transcript of the official stenographic notes of the judge's charge to the jury. The stenographer refused to do so on the order of the trial judge, and the trial judge refused to compel compliance with the newspaper's request on the ground that the press had no special right or privilege not possessed by the ordinary citizen. The New York Appellate Division affirmed upon the ground that one not a party to the criminal proceeding had no clear right to obtain such a transcript if the court stenographer did not want to furnish a copy of the transcript. But the New York Court of Appeals unanimously *reversed*, holding that any member of the public not a party to the criminal proceedings, has an enforceable right to the transcript upon payment of the prescribed fee.

Judge Stanley Fuld opined that

> the Constitution of this State explicitly mandates that ''judicial opinions or decisions shall nevertheless be free for publication by any person'' (Art. VI, Sec. 22). The trial judge's charge to the jury may properly be regarded as a ''decision'' within the ambit of that provision, since the charge embodies the law of the case as decided and declared by the trial court. . . . The clear import of the constitutional mandate is that neither the legislature nor the courts may unreasonably curtail or restrict free access by all persons to judicial opin-

ions and defenses. . . . No other rule is conceivable in a society nurtured on freedom of discussion of matters of public interest. Without access to the official records, the press might well be hampered in reporting opinions or decisions for fear of transgressing the limitations imposed by the law of libel, that the report be a "fair and true" one. To permit a judge to prohibit the stenographer from transcribing or furnishing copies of decisions rendered by him would thwart and tend to nullify the basic purpose of the constitutional safeguard.[40]

The electronic media's broadcasting rights represent, in the words of Justice Brennan, "potentially the most efficient and effective 'marketplace of ideas' ever devised."[41] Indeed recognition of the need for broadcasting criminal trials "rests on the assumption that the widest possible dissemination of information from diverse and antagonistic sources is essential to the welfare of the public, that a free press is a condition of a free society."[42] The prior restraint doctrine[43] precludes court rulings that might proscribe the broadcasting or telecasting of criminal trials. In essence, the dissemination of news or information that has already been gathered or received should not be restricted.[44] Eighteen years ago, in Dorfman v. Meiszner,[45] the Seventh U.S. Court of Appeals held that a trial court rule banning electronic media coverage in the criminal courtroom "or its environs" was an impermissible prior restraint since the rule could be used to ban such coverage in areas that pose no immediate threat to the judicial proceedings. The Washington Supreme Court in State v. Coe[46] dealt with the issue of a radio and television station that was held in contempt by a trial court for violating a court order prohibiting the broadcasting of accurate, lawfully obtained copies of tape recordings that had been played in open court. The prior restraint order, which would otherwise be invalid, "cannot be sustained merely because the trial judge and counsel were pressed for time;" indeed, "in such situations, the heavy presumption of unconstitutionality requires the trial judge to resolve all doubts against 'prior restraint' and to deny requests for such orders," especially where the trial judge "could not possibly know whether 'prior restraint' was strictly and inescapably necessary." The court observed that "the inflections of voice recorded on the tapes themselves constituted substantive information which could not be adequately communicated to the public through the publication of cold transcripts or their reading by actors. Since such information was highly relevant to Coe's two major defenses, broadcasting the tapes served a far greater public interest than mere drama or entertainment.'' Accordingly, the trial court's judgment of contempt was reversed. The dissenting opinion believed that the majority position granted the press and media ''an absolute right to publish and broadcast lawfully obtained information. . . . The notion that any right is absolute conflicts with basic constitutional analysis, delegates unwisely judicial responsibility for protecting individual rights and celebrates the rhetoric of prior restraint over the substantive values inherent in First Amendment analysis.'' The dissent was concerned with the press and media's not judiciously utilizing the evidence presented in court: ''The broadcast of any one of these items (i.e., 'gruesome or obscene photographs and of taped conversations between participants in criminal activity') has the potential for causing irreparable prejudice to a defendant or grievous invasion of a victim's privacy.'' It should be noted that State v. Coe involved out-of-court usage of evidence rather than television coverage of the event itself.

Another restraint on them, argue the press and media, is the so-called ''fairness doctrine'' administered by the FCC. According to the Communications Act of 1934, broadcasters have an obligation ''to operate in the public interest and to afford reasonable opportunity for the discussion of conflicting views on issues of public importance.'' The fairness doctrine includes within its scope a personal attack rule and an equal opportunity rule. The former is triggered when an attack is made on the honesty, character, integrity, or personal qualities of an identified person or group during the presentation of views on a controversial issue of public importance. The broadcaster must notify the attacked person or group within seven days, furnish the attacked person or group with a tape or transcript of the attack, and offer a reasonable opportunity for response. The personal attack rule does not pertain to bona fide news programs, to attacks made by legally qualified candidates for election, or to call-in talk shows. The equal opportunity rule applies only to political candidates. The restraint on press and media is the devotion of a reasonable percentage of broadcast time to the coverage of controversial issues and to the reply to them. In August 1987 the FCC publicly announced that it would no longer enforce the fairness doctrine for it had determined that the doctrine was unconstitutional in violating the First Amendment rights of broadcasters. Yet in 1969 in Red Lion Broadcasting Co. v. FCC[47] the U.S. Supreme

Court had unanimously upheld the doctrine: "Because of the scarcity of radio frequencies, the Government is permitted to put restraints on licensees in favor of others whose views should be expressed on this unique medium. . . . It is the right of the viewers and listeners, not the right of the broadcasters, which is paramount." The FCC has not over the past years been alert to the value of the fairness doctrine. From 1973 to 1976, it received 49,801 complaints on the fairness doctrine but issued inquiries or rulings in only 314 cases. In August 1985, it issued a report concluding that the doctrine was "an unnecessary and detrimental regulatory mechanism" that no longer served the public interest.

NOTES

1. See Chapters 1 and 2 herein.
2. ———NY2d———, ———NE2d——— (June 4, 1987).
3. See Chapter 3 herein.
4. See NYLJ (June 5, 1987) at 1.
5. Dkt 67,352, Florida Supreme Court.
6. ———F Supp——— (SDNY, July 12, 1987).
7. NYLJ (July 13, 1987) at 1 et seq.
8. ———F2d——— (2d Cir., 1987).
9. See New York Times (Sept. 15, 1987) at B4.
10. See generally 4 U Haw L Rev (1982) at p. 94.
11. 1976 Wash U L Q 1 (1976).
12. 408 US 665 (1972).
13. Id. at p. 681.
14. 448 US 555 (1980).
15. Infra note 10 at p. 98.
16. Infra note 14 at p. 575. Earlier in 1978, in Landmark Communications, Inc. v. Virginia, 438 US 829 (1978), Justice Stewart had commented: "There could hardly be a higher governmental interest than a State's interest in the quality of its judiciary" (p. 848).
17. Infra note 14 at p. 576.
18. Id. at pp. 572–73.
19. 436 US 547 (1978).
20. See 94 Harv L Rev 1 (1980) at p. 54.
21. See 85 Colum L Rev 1546 (1985) at 1563.
22. Cf. Westmoreland v. CBS, 752 F2d 16 (2d Cir., 1984), cert den sub nom Cable News Network, Inc. v. U.S. District Court, 105 S Ct 3478 (1985).
23. 753 F2d 617 (7th Cir., 1985).

24. See Okla Code Jud Conduct, Canon 3 (A)(7)(c).
25. See Sup Ct R 81, Canon 3A (7)(c), 17A Ariz Rev Stat Ann (1984).
26. See Cal R Ct 980(b) (1985).
27. See Post-Newsweek Stations, Florida, Inc. v. U.S., 370 So2d 764 (Fla., 1979).
28. 449 US 560 (1981).
29. Id. at p. 581.
30. Infra note 21 at p. 1567.
31. 438 US 1 (1978), rev'g 546 F2d 284 (9th Cir., 1976).
32. Id. at pp. 31–32.
33. See Pell v. Procunier, 417 US 817 (1974).
34. See Sheppard v. Maxwell, 384 US 333 (1966).
35. 408 US 665 (1972).
36. Id. at p. 715.
37. 319 US 141 (1943).
38. Id. at p. 143.
39. 72 NY2d 677, 143 NE2d 256 (1957).
40. Id. at pp. 682, 258.
41. CBS, Inc. v. Democratic National Committee, 412 US 94 (1973) at p. 195.
42. See Associated Press v. United States, 326 US 1 (1945).
43. See Near v. Minnesota, 283 US 697 (1931).
44. See Nebraska Press Assn v. Stuart, 427 US 539 (1976).
45. 430 F2d 558 (7th Cir., 1970).
46. 679 P2d 353 (Wash., 1984).
47. 395 US 367 (1969).

7

Courtroom Cameras, Electronic Media Equipment, and the Trial Lawyer

Cameras and electronic media equipment in the criminal courtroom, it is said, can adversely and pointedly affect the trial lawyer and therefore deprive the accused defendant of his or her right to a fair trial under the Sixth Amendment.[1] The initial decision of the trial lawyer in deciding whether to take the case might be influenced by the prospect of being photographed or being on television. The trial lawyer may be too distracted by the cameras and the electronic media equipment to perform his or her duties properly. He or she may play to the cameras while handling a televised criminal case and act in a manner that will further his or her own, and not necessarily the client's, best interests.[2] According to Post-Newsweek Stations, Florida, Inc. v. U.S.,[3] there is empirical evidence that trial attorneys are aware of, distracted by, and feel nervous before courtroom television cameras to a greater extent than do all other courtroom participants. The contrary argument is that the presence of the camera and electronic media equipment in the criminal courtroom might well make trial attorneys perform with more concern and more efficiency because they are in front of a massive television audience.[4]

There can be little doubt that cameras and electronic media equipment have almost a right to be in the criminal courtroom, subject to the accused's right to a fair trial and subject to reasonable and express restraints of time, place, and manner of operation. As stated in Standard 8-3 of the ABA Standards Relating to Fair Trial and Free Press, the coverage is allowed "in a manner that will be unobtrusive, will not distract or otherwise adversely affect witnesses or other trial participants and will not otherwise interfere with the administration of justice." This standard was adopted by the ABA House of Delegates on August 11, 1982; Canon 3A(7) of the Code of Judicial Conduct was repealed, and new Canon 3A(7), substantially similar to Standard 8-3, was adopted. Undoubtedly, the U.S. Supreme Court decision of Chandler v. Florida[5] prompted the ABA's change of attitude.

The trial lawyer's conduct in the criminal courtroom before cameras and electronic media equipment is governed by many rules of the particular court, as well as by the ABA Model Rules of Professional Conduct, the ABA Standards Relating to Fair Trial and Free Press, the ABA Code of Professional Responsibility, and the ABA Standards for Criminal Justice. For example, Rule 8.2(a) of the ABA Model Rules of Professional Conduct[6] states that "a lawyer shall not make a statement that the lawyer knows to be false or with reckless disregard as to its truth or falsity concerning the qualifications or integrity of a judge, adjudicatory officer or public legal officer." The thrust here is clearly that false statements by a trial attorney can undermine public confidence in the administration of justice and at the same time impair the accused's right to a fair trial.[7] Rule 8.3 mandates that "(a) A lawyer having knowledge that another lawyer has committed a violation of the Rules of Professional Conduct that raises a substantial question as to that lawyer's honesty, trustworthiness, or fitness as a lawyer in other respects, shall inform the appropriate professional authority." And section b mandates the same procedure where "a judge has committed a violation of applicable rules of judicial conduct." Indeed, self-regulation of the legal profession requires that lawyers initiate disciplinary investigations. It should be noted that the term *substantial* refers to the seriousness of the possible offense and not the quantum of evidence of which the lawyer is aware.[8] Rule 8.4 states that it is professional misconduct for a lawyer to

> (a) violate or attempt to violate the Rules of Professional Conduct, knowingly assist or induce another to do so, or do so through the acts of another; (b) commit a criminal act that reflects adversely on the lawyer's honesty, trustworthiness, or fitness as a lawyer in other respects; (c) engage in conduct involving dishonesty, fraud, deceit, or misrepresentation; (d) engage in conduct that is prejudicial to the administration of justice; (e) state or imply an

ability to influence improperly a government agency or official; or (f) knowingly assist a judge or judicial officer in conduct that is a violation of applicable rules of judicial conduct or other law.''

In a similar vein is DR1-102(A) of the ABA Code of Professional Responsibility, providing that a lawyer shall not

(1) violate a Disciplinary Rule; (2) circumvent a Disciplinary Rule through actions of another; (3) engage in illegal conduct involving moral turpitude; (4) engage in conduct involving dishonesty, fraud, deceit, or misrepresentation; (5) engage in conduct that is prejudicial to the administration of justice; and (6) engage in any other conduct that adversely reflects on his fitness to practice law.

Rule 8.5 states that ''a lawyer admitted to practice in this jurisdiction is subject to the disciplinary authority of this jurisdiction although engaged in practice elsewhere.''

The impartiality and decorum of the tribunal is the subject of Rule 3.5 of the Model Rules of Professional Conduct—specifically, that the lawyer shall not ''(a) seek to influence a judge, juror, prospective juror, or other official by means prohibited by law; (b) communicate ex parte with such a person except as permitted by law; or (c) engage in conduct intended to disrupt a tribunal.'' Interestingly, the lawyer may stand firm against abuse by a judge but should avoid reciprocation; the judge's default is no justification for similar dereliction by the lawyer.

DR 7-106 of the ABA Code of Professional Responsibility sets forth the bounds of trial conduct:

(A) A lawyer shall not disregard or advise his client to disregard a standing rule of a tribune or a ruling of a tribunal made in the course of a proceeding, but he may take appropriate steps in good faith to test the validity of such rule or ruling. (B) In presenting a matter to a tribunal a lawyer shall disclose: (1) legal authority in the controlling jurisdiction known to him to be directly adverse to the position of his client and which is not disclosed by opposing counsel; and (2) unless privileged or irrelevant, the identities of the clients he represents and of the persons who employed him. (C) In appearing in his professional capacity before a tribunal a lawyer shall not: (1) state or allude to any matter that he has no reasonable basis to believe is relevant to the case or that will not be supported by admissible evidence; (2) ask any question that he has no reasonable basis to believe is relevant to the case and that is intended to degrade a witness or other person; (3) assert his personal knowledge of the facts in issue, except when testifying as a witness; (4) assert his personal opinion as to the justness of a cause, as to the credibility of a witness, as to the culpability of a civil litigant, or as to the guilt or innocence of an accused; but he may argue, on his analysis of the evidence, for any position or conclusion with respect to the matters stated therein; (5) fail to comply with known local customs of courtesy or practice of the bar or a particular tribunal without giving to opposing counsel timely notice of his intent not to comply; (6) engage in undignified or discourteous conduct which is degrading to a tribunal; and (7) intentionally or habitually violate any established rule of procedure or of evidence.[9]

Standards 8-2.1, 8-2.2, and 8-2.3 of the ABA Standards Relating to Fair Trial and Free Press concern the conduct of law enforcement officers, judges, and court personnel in criminal cases with respect to the release or disclosure of information that might be prejudicial to the right of the public or of the accused to a fair trial.[10] The government can set restraints on its own employees that could not constitutionally be imposed on a private citizen. Obviously the trial attorney is not bound thereby even in his or her role as a law enforcement officer, even if being paid out of public funds. It is arguable whether the prosecuting attorney is a public employee first and a trial attorney second with respect to such restraints on conduct and speech. Standard 8-2.1(b) deals with photographing, televising, and interviewing persons in custody. The possibility of prejudice to the suspect or the accused is substantial, and therefore under no circumstances can a person in custody be forced to pose for the camera or to submit to an interview by representatives of the press or media.[11] Standard 8-2.2 with respect to disclosures by court personnel is similar but not so detailed as the restraints imposed under Standard 8-2.1 for law enforcement officers. Standard 8-2.3 on the conduct of judges is clearly an unequivocal axiom of the administration of justice.

Just as the trial lawyer can be adversely affected by the presence of the camera and electronic media equipment in the criminal courtroom, so may the witnesses and the jury be at the mercy of the intruding equipment. Justice Clark in Estes v. Texas[12] listed four possible ways that the presence of such equipment could prejudice jurors against the criminally accused: (1) jurors may be pressured into reaching a verdict that conforms to community opinion of the accused; (2) their awareness of the cameras may distract and prevent them from giving the trial testimony the full time and attention that trial testimony requires; (3) if they are not sequestered, they may see television broadcasts of the criminal trial and be improperly influenced by what they see in the telecast; and (4) they will form opinions as to defendant's guilt or innocence, thereby jeopardizing new trials if necessary. Witnesses also might feel pressured into giving testimony that conforms to the community opinion of the accused; televising the criminal trial might deter testimony of witnesses who object to the public "circus."[13]

A photograph or a kinescope or videoscope of the criminal proceedings might be a valuable asset in those rare situations where courts do not publish their opinions. For example, the vast majority of the decisions of the Kentucky Court of Appeals are not published.[14] Such unpublished opinions may not be cited as authority in any court in Kentucky, yet they do influence trial judges and attorneys practicing in that state. But an attorney in Kentucky who cites an unpublished opinion to a court may be subject to professional discipline if the violation is intentional or results in injury to his or her client.[15]

NOTES

1. See Chapter 3 herein.

2. See 4 U Haw L Rev (1982) at p. 114.

3. 370 So2d 764 (Fla., 1979) at pp. 768–69.

4. See In re Hearings Concerning Canon 35, 296 P2d 465 (Colo., 1956) at pp. 469–70.

5. 449 US 560 (1981).

6. See generally 46 Ohio St L J 1 (1985). The rules were adopted by the ABA House of Delegates on August 2, 1983. Only Arizona and New Jersey adopted the rules within the first year, 1984.

7. Cf. DR8-102 of the ABA Code of Professional Responsibility.

8. Note that DR1-103(A) of the ABA Code of Professional Responsibility necessitates that "a lawyer possessing unprivileged knowlege of a violation of [a disciplinary rule] shall report such knowledge to . . . authority empowered to investigate or act upon such violation.

9. See generally 38 Tex L Rev 107 (1959). Also Colton v. United States, 306 F2d 633 (2d Cir., 1962) on identification of client.

10. Standard 8-2.1, Release of Information by Law Enforcement Agencies:

> The following regulations should be made effective in each jurisdiction:
>
> (a) A regulation governing the release of information relating to the commission of crimes and to their investigation, prior to the making of an arrest, issuance of an arrest

warrant, or the filing of formal charges. This regulation should establish appropriate procedures for the release of information. It should further provide that, when a crime is believed to have been committed, pertinent facts relating to the crime itself and to investigative procedures may properly be made available, but the identity of a suspect prior to arrest and the results of investigative procedures shall not be disclosed except to the extent necessary to aid in the investigation, to assist in the apprehension of the suspect, or to warn the public of any dangers.

(b) A regulation prohibiting:

(i) The deliberate posing of a person in custody for photographing or televising by representatives of the news media, and

(ii) the interviewing by representatives of the news media of a person in custody except upon request or consent by that person to an interview after being informed adequately of the right to consult with counsel and of the right to refuse to grant an interview.

(c) A regulation providing as follows:

From the commencement of the investigation of a criminal matter until the completion of a trial or disposition without trial, a law enforcement officer within this agency shall not release or authorize the release of any extrajudicial statement, for dissemination by any means of public communication, if such statement poses a clear and present danger to the fairness of the trial. In no event, however, shall a law enforcement officer make an extrajudicial statement concerning the following matters:

(i) the existence or contents of any confession, admission or statement given by the accused, or the refusal or failure of the accused to make a statement, and

(ii) the possibility of a plea of guilty to the offense charged or a lesser offense or other disposition.

Consistent with the clear and present danger standard in paragraph (c), a law enforcement officer may be subject to disciplinary action with respect to extrajudicial statements concerning the following matters:

(A) the prior criminal record (including arrests, indictments, or other charges of crime), the character or reputation of the accused, or any opinion as to the accused's guilt or innocence or as to the merits of the case or the evidence in the case;

(B) the performance of any examination or tests, or the accused's refusal or failure to submit to an examination or test;

(C) the identity, testimony, or credibility of prospective witnesses; and

(D) information which the law enforcement officer knows or has reason to know would be inadmissible as evidence in a trial.

(d) A regulation authorizing a law enforcement officer at any time:

(i) to make a factual statement of the accused's name, age, residence, occupation, and family status, and, if the accused has not been apprehended, to release any further information necessary to aid in the accused's apprehension or to warn the public of any dangers that may exist;

(ii) to announce the fact and circumstances of arrest, including the time and place of arrest, resistance, pursuit, and use of weapons;

(iii) to announce the identity of the investigating and arresting officer or agency and length of the investigation;

(iv) to announce the identity of the victim or complainant if the release of that information is not otherwise prohibited by law;

(v) to make an announcement, at the time of seizure of any physical evidence (other than a confession, admission, or statement), which is limited to a description of the evidence seized;

(vi) to disclose the nature, substance or text of the charge, including a brief description of the offense charged;

(vii) to quote from or refer without comment to public records of the court of the case;

(viii) to announce the scheduling or result of any stage in the judicial process; and

(ix) to request assistance in obtaining evidence.

(e) A regulation providing for the enforcement of the foregoing rules by the imposition of appropriate disciplinary sanctions.

Nothing in this standard is intended to preclude any law enforcement officer from replying to charges of misconduct that are publicly made against him or her or from participating in any legislative, administrative, or investigative hearing, nor is this standard intended to supersede more restrictive rules governing the release of information concerning juvenile offenders.

11. Standard 8-2.2, Disclosures by Court Personnel:

Court personnel shall not disclose to any unauthorized person information relating to a pending criminal case that is not part of the public records of the court and that may be prejudicial to the right of the people or the defendant to a fair trial. Particular reference should be made in this rule to standards 8-3.2 and 8-1. Appropriate disciplinary action should be provided for infractions of this rule.

Standard 8-2.3, Conduct of Judges:

Judges should refrain from any conduct or the making of any statements that may be prejudicial to the right of the people or of the defendant to a fair trial.

12. 381 US 532 (1965).
13. See 4 U Haw L Rev (1982) at pp. 113–14.
14. See generally 73 Ky L J (1984–1985) at pp. 145 et seq.
15. See Model Code of Professional Responsibility Dr 7-101(A)(3).

8

Prejudicial Trial Publicity and the Conduct of the Trial Lawyer

It was probably in 1966 in Sheppard v. Maxwell[1] that the U.S. Supreme Court for the first time expressed its unabiding concern for prejudicial trial publicity in criminal cases. Rather than await reversal on appellate review of the trial court proceedings, the Court mandated that primary responsibility rests on trial judges to take decisive action to neutralize from the beginning the effects of prejudicial publicity in criminal cases. The Court ordered lower courts to "take such steps by rule and regulation that will protect their processes from prejudicial outside interferences," noting especially that "extrajudicial statements by an lawyer . . . which divulged prejudicial matters" could be proscribed and that "neither prosecutors, counsel for the defense, nor the accused . . . should be permitted to frustrate [a court's] function." The accused's right to a fair trial under the Sixth Amendment was uppermost in the minds of the Court.[2] Justice Brennan in Nebraska Press Association[3] later analyzed the role of trial attorneys:

> As officers of the court, court personnel and attorneys have a fiduciary responsibility not to engage in public debate that will redound to the detriment of the accused or that will obstruct the fair administration of justice. It is very doubtful that the court would not have the power to control release of information by these individuals in appropriate cases and to impose suitable limitations whose transgressions could result in disciplinary proceedings.[4]

The ABA, in promulgating and amending its Standards Relating to Fair Trial and Free Press, was particularly mindful of the Sixth Amendment's right to a public and a fair trial rather than the First Amendment's right of access for the public and the press and media to the criminal courtroom. It was in 1908 that the ABA had first clamored against lawyers' "trying their cases in the newspapers." Canon 20 of the ABA Canons of Professional Ethics eighty years ago stated that

> it is unprofessional for a lawyer to make or to sanction the issuance or use by another, of any press release, statement, or other disclosure of information, whether of alleged facts or of opinion, for release to the public by newspaper . . . relating to any pending or anticipated . . . criminal prosecution, the purpose or effect of which may be to prejudice or interfere with a fair trial in the courts or with the due administration of justice.[5]

Rule 3.6 of the ABA Model Rules of Professional Conduct, delineating trial publicity, is a remarkable document skirting the Scylla and Charybdis of the right to a fair trial and the right of free expression.[6] It adopts the general criterion of "substantial likelihood of materially prejudicing an adjudicative hearing" to describe impermissible conduct of trial attorneys. (The 1986 New York case of National Broadcasting Co. v. Cooperman[7] rejected that criterion in favor of a "reasonable likelihood" standard. The court held that a trial judge, before imposing a gag order, must find less restrictive alternatives insufficient; and even then, the court order must be tailored to prohibit only those statements that "present a reasonable likelihood of a serious threat to a defendant's right to a fair trial.") Rule 3.6, however, omits reference to permitting a trial attorney, at the time of a seizure, to reveal a description of the physical evidence seized.[8] Rule 3.6 does require the giving of fair notice of conduct ordinarily posing unacceptable dangers to the fair administration of justice. The formula in Rule 3.6 is based on the ABA Code of Professional Responsibility and the ABA Standards Relating to Fair Trial and Free Press, as amended.

DR 7-107 of the ABA Code of Professional Responsibility is an extensive document[9] on trial publicity that in its first four sections incorporates the fair trial-free press standards that apply to lawyers as adopted by the ABA House of Delegates in 1968. As spelled out by the New York court in Markfield v. Association of the Bar of the City of New York,[10] the provision of DR 7-107 restricting the right of prosecutor and defense counsel to make extrajudicial statements during trial is to prevent an attorney associated with a criminal trial from making statements or disseminating matter that have the likelihood of interfering with the fair administration of justice. DR 7-107 seeks to achieve a fair balance between an attorney's right of free speech and society's interest in protecting the integrity of the judicial process and thereby guaranteeing a fair and impartial criminal trial.

The New York court here deemed the disciplinary rule not to be a violation of free speech under the First Amendment. The professional disciplinary rule would be unconstitutional if interpreted as an all-out gag restraint relating to the trial regardless of its effect or lack of effect on the trial. Indeed, the rule, to be constitutional, must achieve a fair balance between the lawyer's right of free speech and society's interest in protecting the integrity of the judicial processes, thereby guaranteeing a fair and impartial trial. Application of the rule by the New York court in 1975 was limited to those situations where it is found that extrajudicial statements did present a "clear and present danger" to the administration of justice. The New York appellate court in the Markfield case[11] annulled a determination that an attorney violated Dr 7-107 because of his participation in a radio panel discussion concerning prison rebellions during the time a criminal trial was in progress. The court observed that there was no evidence to indicate that the extrajudicial statements the attorney made were reasonably likely to interfere with a fair trial, and therefore the statements did not justify the imposition of any disciplinary sanction, informal or otherwise.

The Seventh U.S. Court of Appeals in In Re Oliver[12] took the view that any restriction on the attorney's right of free speech must be of such a nature that it would present serious and imminent threat to the administration of justice. Here the attorney had simply announced publicly that he was not going to obey the policy of the federal district court not to comment on pending court matters. Several courts have held that attorney discipline is appropriate if there is a reasonable likelihood of prejudice to a fair trial. In Hirschkop v. the Virginia State Bar,[13] the federal district court in Virginia stated that DR 7-107 struck a reasonable balance between fair trial and free speech and constituted a reasonable regulation as to time, manner, and place.[14] The Fourth

U.S. Court of Appeals[15] affirmed and reversed in part, pointing out that (1) the attorney had standing to bring the suit; (2) the rule did not violate First Amendment rights of attorneys insofar as the rule applied to criminal trials; (3) the rule was not constitutionally infirm because of its failure to limit the ban on lawyers' comments to those instances where the comments posed a serious and imminent threat to a fair trial; (4) certain provisions of the rule, however, were void for vagueness; (5) the rule was unconstitutionally overbroad insofar as it restricted the comments that could be made by lawyers associated with civil litigation; and (6) the part of the rule that dealt with administrative hearings was also unconstitutional by reason of being overbroad. The federal appellate court was deeply divided in its ruling; one judge concurred in the per curiam ruling, three judges concurred in part and dissented in part, and three separate opinions were written.

In Chicago Council of Lawyers v. Bauer,[16] the Seventh U.S. Court of Appeals reemphasized that a serious and imminent threat to the administration of justice or a "clear and present danger" must exist before imposing discipline on the trial attorney. The court ruled that the federal district court rules on no comment restricted communications other than those that posed a serious and imminent threat to the administration of justice. The court opined:

> We are of the view that the rubric used in the rules under consideration, that lawyers' comments about pending or imminent litigation must be proscribed "if there is a reasonable likelihood that such dissemination will interfere with a fair trial or otherwise prejudice the due administration of justice" is overbroad and therefore does not meet constitutional standards. Instead, we think a narrower and more restrictive standard, the one formulated in *Chase v. Robson*, 435 F.2d 1059, 1061-62 (7th Cir. 1970), and reaffirmed in *In re Oliver*, 452 F.2d 111 (7th Cir. 1971), should apply: Only those comments that pose a "serious and imminent threat" of interference with the fair administration of justice can be constitutionally proscribed. Given the objectives of clearness, precision, and narrowness we are of the view that this formulation is more in keeping with the precepts announced by the Supreme Court to which we have alluded than the one used by the local rules of the district court. A lawyer is put on stricter notice if he must gauge his intended comments by a test that limits only comments which are a serious and imminent threat of interference with a fair trial than if his statements were governed by the more amorphous phrase: "a reasonable likelihood that such comment will interfere with a fair trial."

We should emphasize at this point, however, that this standard is not constitutionally sufficient by itself. While the application of the standard to these rules can eliminate overbreadth, the specific rules are also necessary in order to avoid vagueness. The rules furnish the context necessary to determine what may constitute a "serious and imminent threat" of interference with the fair administration of justice.

The court continued:

The barring of comment by lawyers representing criminal defendants may seem questionable for a variety of other reasons. The Sixth Amendment speaks only of the right of an accused and the Fifth Amendment only of the right of persons and not of the Government. The publication of the fact that a person is under investigation or is charged with the commission of a crime makes it difficult for the person involved to counter any injury to himself, his family, or friends caused by the publicity if his attorney is allowed only to say without elaboration that his client maintains his innocence. Under the no-comment rules, the lawyer, who usually is more articulate and more knowledgeable in the law than the accused, can perhaps best speak about such matters as defenses or the reputation of the accused as a law-abiding citizen. Only slight reflection is needed to realize that the scales of justice in the eyes of the public are weighed extraordinarily heavy against an accused after his indictment. A bare denial and a possible reminder that a charged person is presumed to be innocent until proven guilty is often insufficient to balance the scales.

Regardless of these considerations and our disquietude, we nonetheless believe that certain proscriptions on speech can constitutionally be invoked against defense counsel. We must not forget that public justice is no less important than an accused's right to a fair trial.[17]

But in Waldo v. Lakeshore Estates, Inc.[18] the court rule regulating class actions that forbade all parties and their counsel in potential and actual class actions under Rule 23 of the Federal Rules of Civil Procedure (FRCP) from communicating with any potential or actual class member not a formal party to the instant action, without the consent and approval of the court, was deemed not to be too broad nor violative of the First Amendment. The same court rule specifically forbade communications involving the solicitation of legal representation of potential and actual class members who were not formal parties, communications involving the solicitation of fees and expenses and agreements to pay fees and expenses, as well as communications from counsel or a party that might tend to misrepresent the status, purposes, and effects of the action. In essence, the court opined that the rule effectuated a compelling and substantial governmental interest rooted in the judiciary, the bar, and the public at large.

Other disciplinary rules govern communication with or investigation of jurors,[19] contact with witnesses,[20] and contact with officials.[21] ABA Standards Relating to Fair Trial and Free Press provide much guidance for trial attorneys in the criminal proceeding, whether as prosecutor or defense counsel. Standard 3-1.3, for example, relates to public statements by prosecutors[22] and emphasizes the prosecutor's responsibility to the administration of justice: nothing shall be done that will impair the right of the accused to fair and impartial treatment in every case. Personal aggrandizement is prohibited; circumspection in this regard is most acutely required, especially in cases that excite the public interest. Standard 4-1.3 describes public statements by defense counsel; avoidance of personal publicity and compliance with all other standards is mandatory.[23] Personal aggrandizement operates only to the detriment of a particular client and is demeaning of the proper role of defense counsel. Standard 8-1.1 is a comprehensive document on the conduct of all attorneys in criminal cases, with special reference to extrajudicial statements.[24] Paragraph a states the general duty of the attorney to promote trial fairness in criminal cases in which the attorney is involved. The standard is applicable from the beginning of the criminal investigation until the sentencing or release of the accused from custody. Standard 8-1.1 assigns great weight to the attorney's right under the First Amendment to make public, extrajudicial statements about criminal investigations or criminal litigation.[25] Violation of Standard 8-1.1 turns on proof that the extrajudicial statement would pose a clear and present danger to the fairness of the criminal trial[26] or a reasonable likelihood of interference with a fair trial.[27]

The reasonable likelihood criterion has been challenged as overly restrictive on First Amendment rights of trial attorneys.[28] The U.S. Supreme Court in its 1978 decision in Landmark Communications, Inc. v. Virginia[29] advanced four prerequisites to any restraint on public comment of trial attorneys: (1) the restraint advances a legitimate governmental interest; (2) the public comment poses an extremely serious threat to a governmental interest sought to be protected by the restraint; (3) the threat to that governmental interest appears likely to occur imminently; and (4) the restraint on public comment is necessary to secure protection or advancement of the governmental interest that is in jeopardy. All four prerequisites are part and parcel of the "clear and present danger" rule[30] and also essential elements of the "serious and imminent" threat test set forth in the Chicago Council of Lawyers case.[31] Note that the burden of proof to show a violation of Standard 8-1.1 rests on the party charging a breach of the standard, despite the contrary language in the Chicago Council of Lawyers case, which reformulated DR 7-107.

Paragraph c of Standard 8-1.1 enumerates information categories that the trial attorney is free to release without risk of sanction. Obviously the general prohibition of paragraph a does not apply to the release of such information because it is deemed that the threat to trial fairness is minimal. Paragraph d delineates restrictions on the release of information about juvenile proceedings, as well as the First Amendment right to reply of the attorney charged publicly with misconduct.[32]

Standard 8-1.2 states that "unless adopted by statute or pursuant to the supervisory authority of the highest court in the jurisdiction, the substance of Standard 8-1.1 should be adopted as a rule of court governing the conduct of attorneys." Standard 8-1.3 declares that "violation of Standard 8-1.1 shall be grounds for judicial and bar disciplinary action. Any attorney or bar association shall have standing to petition an appropriate court for the institution of disciplinary proceedings, and the court may initiate such proceedings on its own motion." Standard 8-1.3 thus describes the method of enforcement of Standard 8-1.1, and contempt proceedings are therefore not appropriate for violations of Standard 8-1.1. Generally professional discipline—reprimand, suspension, or disbarment—is suffice.[33]

Courts have also promulgated their own rules on restrictions on public statements by trial attorneys. Local Rule 7(a) of the U.S. District Courts for the Eastern and Southern Districts of New York, according to the Federal Bar Council in 1987, allegedly gives the prosecution an unfair advantage over defense counsel.[34] Despite the ban on prosecutors and defense lawyers alike from making any public comment that poses "a reasonable likelihood" of interfering with a fair trial or otherwise prejudicing the due administration of justice, the Federal Bar Council proposed that prior to arrest or indictment of the accused, defense attorneys should also be relieved of any restraints in dealing with the press and media. The council was also concerned with the privilege accorded prosecutors to refer without comment to the detailed indictment, which is a public record filed in the case. The advantage stems from the prosecutor's control over the record. The defense counsel can only announce without comment that the accused denies the charges in the detailed indictment.

The Ninth U.S. Court of Appeals in Levine v. U.S. District Court[35] had observed that

> with the nearness of trial, the potential for prejudice becomes particularly acute. There's nothing in the [California] Code of Professional Responsibility requiring or even recommending that an attorney argue his or her case in the press or on the courthouse steps. Neither the press nor the public has the right to hear counsel argue their case prior to this court, and the impaneled jury hearing the evidence, when doing so seriously impedes the fair and effective administration of justice.

The federal appellate court here enumerated the following subjects of public statements that should have been curbed by defense counsel:

> the character, credibility or reputation of a party; the identity of a witness or the expected testimony of a party or a witness; statements of admissions given by a defendant or defendant's refusal or failure to make the statements or admissions; the identity or nature of physical evidence expected to be presented or the absence of such physical evidence; the strengths or weaknesses of the case of either party; and any other information the lawyer knows or reasonably should know is likely to be inadmissible as evidence and would create a substantial risk of prejudice if disclosed.

The concurring opinion of Judge Sneed argued that "there is no need to shelter jurors from what the press reports about the statements of counsel before and during the trial." A note writer in *St. Mary's Law Journal* concludes:

> Many of those who have argued against the imposition of restrictions on comments by defense counsel have succumbed to the mischievous tendency whereby beguiling formulas of respect for the First Amendment are made to do service for critical analysis by being turned into dogma. Indeed, more often than not, the arguments against restrictions are little more than panegyrics to the First Amendment rather than sound and dispassionate analyses.[36]

In May 1978, the Federal Bar Association issued a report that recommended greater freedom for defense counsel to tell the press and media about their cases before courts in the New York City area.[37] According to the report, "Existing rules concerning attorneys' extrajudicial statements conflict with the First Amendment rights of defense counsel and their clients."[38] In urging revision of existing rules, the report proclaimed that "specific prohibitions apply only to the prosecution and defense counsel [should not be] . . . limited to the public record and a terse announcement that the accused denies the charges." On the other hand, the Bronx County, New York, prosecutor, Mario Merola, has been civilly sued on two occasions for statements made to the press and media outside the criminal courtroom. In Martin v. Merola,[39] six men indicted on an alleged loansharking operation in 1974 sued him under a civil rights statute accusing Merola of linking them to "Mafia crime families" and calling them "vultures." The Second U.S. Court of Appeals in 1976 dismissed the case as premature because of the pending criminal action,[40] although two judges warned that excessive statements by a prosecutor could be actionable. In 1987 in Schiavone Construction Co. v. Merola,[41] the suit was brought by former U.S. Secretary of Labor Raymond Donovan whose construction company (and himself) were acquitted by a jury of charges of defrauding the New York City Transit Authority of $7.4 million. Merola was accused of stating, "Donovan has a staff of 15 lawyers, some of the best in the country. He also has a public relations firm working in his behalf. The lawyers are throwing handfuls of darts in the form of motions at the federal and state courts. He just needs to have one stick. Would an innocent guy need all that help?"[42] And in Powers v. McGuigan,[43] the Second U.S. Court of Appeals ruled that alleged leaks by the prosecutor to the press and media did not adversely affect the fairness of trial.

NOTES

1. 384 US 333 (1966).
2. See Chapter 3 herein.
3. 427 US 539 (1976).
4. Id. at p. 601.
5. See Warren Freedman, "New Media Coverage of Criminal Cases and the Right to a Fair Trial," 40 Neb L Rev 391 (1961).
6. Rule 3.6, Trial Publicity:

(a) A lawyer shall not make an extrajudicial statement that a reasonable person would expect to be disseminated by means of public communication if the lawyer knows or reasonably should know that it will have a substantial likelihood of materially prejudicing an adjudicative proceeding.

(b) A statement referred to in paragraph (a) ordinarily is likely to have such an effect when it refers to a civil matter triable to a jury, a criminal matter, or any other proceeding that could result in incarceration, and the statement relates to:

(1) the character, credibility, reputation or criminal record of a party, suspect in a criminal investigation or witness, or the identity of a witness, or the expected testimony of a party or witness;

(2) in a criminal case or proceeding that could result in incarceration, the possibility of a plea of guilty to the offense or the existence or contents of any confession, admission, or statement given by a defendant or suspect or that person's refusal or failure to make a statement;

(3) the performance or results of any examination or test or the refusal or failure of a person to submit to an examination or test, or the identity or nature of physical evidence expected to be presented;

(4) any opinion as to the guilt or innocence of a defendant or suspect in a criminal case or proceeding that could result in incarceration;

(5) information the lawyer knows or reasonably should know is likely to be inadmissible as evidence in a trial and would if disclosed create a substantial risk of prejudicing an impartial trial; or

(6) the fact that a defendant has been charged with a crime, unless there is included therein a statement explaining that the charge is merely an accusation and that the defendant is presumed innocent until and unless proven guilty.

(c) Notwithstanding paragraphs (a) and (b)(1-5), a lawyer involved in the investigation or litigation of a matter may state without elaboration,

(1) the general nature of the claim or defense;

(2) the information contained in a public record;

(3) that an investigation of the matter is in progress, including the general scope of the investigation, the offense or claim or defense involved and, except when prohibited by law, the identity of the persons involved;

(4) the scheduling or result of any step in litigation;

(5) a request for assistance in obtaining evidence and information necessary thereto;

(6) a warning of danger concerning the behavior of a person involved, when there is reason to believe that there exists the likelihood of substantial harm to an individual or to the public interest; and

(7) in a criminal case;

(i) the identity, residence, occupation and family status of the accused;

(ii) if the accused has not been apprehended, information necessary to aid in apprehension of that person;

(iii) the fact, time and place of arrest; and

(iv) the identity of investigating and arresting officers or agencies and the length of the investigation.

7. 501 NYS2d 405 (2d Dept., 1986).

8. See DR 7-107(C)(7) of the ABA Code of Professional Responsibility, which is otherwise similar to Rule 3.6.

9. DR 7-107, Trial Publicity:

(A) A lawyer participating in or associated with the investigation of a criminal matter shall not make or participate in making an extrajudicial statement that a reasonable person would expect to be disseminated by means of public communication and that does more than state without elaboration;

(1) Information contained in a public record.

(2) That the investigation is in progress.

(3) The general scope of the investigation including a description of the offense and, if permitted by law, the identity of the victim.

(4) A request for assistance in apprehending a suspect or assistance in other matters and the information necessary thereto.

(5) A warning to the public of any dangers.

(B) A lawyer or firm associated with the prosecution or defense of a criminal matter shall not, from the time of the filing of a complaint, information, or indictment, the issuance of an arrest warrant, or arrest until the commencement of the trial or disposition without trial, make or participate in making an extrajudicial statement that a reasonable person would expect to be disseminated by means of public communication and that relates to:

(1) The character, reputation, or prior criminal record (including arrests, indictments, or other charges of crime) of the accused.

(2) The possibility of a plea of guilty to the offense charged or to a lesser offense.

(3) The existence or contents of any confession, admission, or statement given by the accused or his refusal or failure to make a statement.

(4) The performance or results of any examinations or tests or the refusal or failure of the accused to submit to examinations or tests.

(5) The identity, testimony, or credibility of a prospective witness.

(6) Any opinion as to the guilt or innocence of the accused, the evidence, or the merits of the case.

(C) DR 7-107(B) does not preclude a lawyer during such period from announcing:

(1) The name, age, residence, occupation, and family status of the accused.

(2) If the accused has not been apprehended, any information necessary to aid in his apprehension or to warn the public of any dangers he may present.

(3) A request for assistance in obtaining evidence.

(4) The identity of the victim of the crime.

(5) The fact, time, and place of arrest, resistance, pursuit, and use of weapons.

(6) The identity of investigating and arresting officers or agencies and the length of the investigation.

(7) At the time of seizure, a description of the physical evidence seized, other than a confession, admission, or statement.

(8) The nature, substance, or text of the charge.

(9) Quotations from or references to public records of the court in the case.

(10) The scheduling or result of any step in the judicial proceedings.

(11) That the accused denies the charges made against him.

(D) During the selection of a jury or the trial of a criminal matter, a lawyer or law firm associated with the prosecution or defense of a criminal matter shall not make or participate in making an extrajudicial statement that a reasonable person would expect to be disseminated by means of public communication and that relates to the trial, parties, or issues in the trial or other matters that are reasonably likely to interfere with a fair trial, except that he may quote from or refer without comment to public records of the court in the case.

(E) After the completion of a trial or disposition without trial of a criminal matter and prior to the imposition of sentence, a lawyer or law firm associated with the prosecution or defense shall not make or participate in making an extrajudicial statement that a reasonable person would expect to be disseminated by public communication and that is reasonably likely to affect the imposition of sentence.

(F) The foregoing provisions of DR 7-107 also apply to professional disciplinary proceedings and juvenile disciplinary proceedings when pertinent and consistent with other law applicable to such proceedings.

(G) A lawyer or law firm associated with a civil action shall not during its investigation or litigation make or participate in making an extrajudicial statement, other than a quotation from or reference to public records, that a reasonable person would expect to be disseminated by means of public communication and that relates to:

(1) Evidence regarding the occurrence or transaction involved.

(2) The character, credibility, or criminal record of a party, witness, or prospective witness.

(3) The performance or results of any examinations or tests or the refusal or failure of a party to submit to such.

(4) His opinion as to the merits of the claims or defenses of a party, except as required by law or administrative rule.

(5) Any other matter reasonably likely to interfere with a fair trial of the action.

(H) During the pendency of an administrative proceeding, a lawyer or law firm associated therewith shall not make or participate in making a statement, other than a quotation from or reference to public records, that a reasonable person would expect to be disseminated by means of public communication if it is made outside the official course of the proceeding and relates to:

(1) Evidence regarding the occurrence or transaction involved.

(2) The character, credibility, or criminal record of a party, witness, or prospective witness.

(3) Physical evidence or the performance or results of any examinations or tests or the refusal or failure of a party to submit to such.

(4) His opinion as to the merits of the claims, defenses, or positions of an interested person.

(5) Any other matter reasonably likely to interfere with a fair hearing.

(I) The foregoing provisions of DR 7-107 do not preclude a lawyer from replying to charges of misconduct publicly made against him or from participating in the proceedings of legislative, administrative, or other investigative bodies.

(J) A lawyer shall exercise reasonable care to prevent his employees and associates from making an extrajudicial statement that he would be prohibited from making under DR 7-107.

10. 370 NYS2d 82 (1975).
11. Id.
12. 452 F2d 111 (7th Cir., 1971).

13. 421 F Supp 1137 (Va., 1976).

14. See In Re Rachmiel, 449 A2d 505 (N.J., 1982).

15. 594 F2d 356 (4th Cir., 1979) sub nom Hirschkop v. Snead.

16. 522 F2d 242 (7th Cir., 1975), cert den 427 US 912 (1976).

17. The court appended to its opinions a copy of Rule 1.07 of the District Court's Local Criminal Rules; Public Discussion by Attorneys of Pending or Imminent Criminal Litigation:

(a) It is the duty of the United States Attorney, or a lawyer or law firm not to release or authorize the release of information or opinion which a reasonable person would expect to be disseminated by means of public communication, in connection with pending or imminent criminal litigation with which he or the firm is associated, if there is a reasonable likelihood that such dissemination will interfere with a fair trial or otherwise prejudice the due administration of justice.

(b) With respect to a grand jury or other pending investigation of any criminal matter, the United States Attorney or a lawyer participating in or associated with the investigation shall refrain from making any extrajudicial statement which a reasonable person would expect to be disseminated by means of public communication, that goes beyond the public record or that is not necessary to inform the public that the investigation is underway, to describe the general scope of the investigation, to obtain assistance in the apprehension of a suspect, to warn the public of any dangers, or otherwise to aid in the investigation.

(c) From the time of arrest, issuance of an arrest warrant, or the filing of a complaint, information, or indictment in any criminal matter until the commencement of trial or disposition without trial, the United States Attorney, or a lawyer or law firm associated with the prosecution or defense shall not release or authorize the release of any extrajudicial statement which a reasonable person would expect to be disseminated by means of public communication, relating to that matter and concerning:

> (1) The prior criminal record (including arrests, indictments, or other charges of crime), or the character or reputation of the accused, except that the lawyer or law firm may make a factual statement of the accused's name, age, residence, occupation, and family status, and if the accused has not been apprehended, the United States Attorney may release any information necessary to aid in his apprehension or to warn the public of any dangers he may present;
>
> (2) The existence or contents of any confession, admission, or statement given by the accused, or the refusal or failure of the accused to make any statement;
>
> (3) The performance of any examinations or tests or the accused's refusal or failure to submit to an examination or test;
>
> (4) The identity, testimony, or credibility of prospective witnesses, except that the lawyer or law firm may announce the identity of the victim if the announcement is not otherwise prohibited by law;
>
> (5) The possibility of a plea of guilty to the offense charged or a lesser offense;
>
> (6) Any opinion as to the accused's guilt or innocence or as to the merits of the case or the evidence in the case.

The foregoing shall not be construed to preclude the United States Attorney, or a lawyer or law firm during this period, in the proper discharge of his or its official or professional obligations, from announcing the fact and circumstances of arrest (including time and place of arrest, resistance, pursuit, and use of weapons), the identity of the investigating and arresting officer or agency, and the length of the investigation; from making an announcement, at the time of seizure of any physical evidence other than a confession, admission or statement, which is limited to a description of the evidence seized; from disclosing the nature, substance, or text of the charge, including a brief description of the offense charged; from quoting or referring without comment to public records of the court in the case; from announcing the scheduling or result of any stage in the judicial process; from requesting assistance in obtaining evidence; or from announcing without further comment that the accused denies the charges made against him.

(d) During the trial of any criminal matter including the period of selection of the jury, no United States Attorney, or lawyer or law firm associated with the prosecution or defense shall give or authorize any extrajudicial statement or interview, relating to the trial or the parties or issues in the trial which a reasonable person would expect to be disseminated by means of public communication, except that the United States Attorney, or lawyer or law firm may quote from or refer without comment to public records of the court in the case.

(e) After the completion of a trial or disposition without trial of any criminal matter, and prior to the imposition of sentence, the United States Attorney, or a lawyer or law firm associated with the prosecution or defense shall refrain from making or authorizing any extrajudicial statement which a reasonable person would expect to be disseminated by means of public communication if there is a resonable likelihood that such dissemination will affect the imposition of sentence. (Amended effective March 9th, 1971)

18. 433 F Supp 782 (La., 1977), dism 579 F2d 642 (5th Cir., 1978).

19. DR 7-108, Communication with or Investigation of Jurors:

(A) Before the trial of a case a lawyer connected therewith shall not communicate with or cause another to communicate with anyone he knows to be a member of the venire from which the jury will be selected for the trial of the case.

(B) During the trial of a case:

(1) A lawyer connected therewith shall not communicate with or cause another to communicate with any member of the jury.

(2) A lawyer who is not connected therewith shall not communicate with or cause to communicate with a juror concerning the case.

(C) DR 7-108 (A) and (B) do not prohibit a lawyer from communicating with veniremen or jurors in the course of official proceedings.

(D) After discharge of the jury from further consideration of a case with which the lawyer was connected, the lawyer shall not ask questions of or make comments to a member of that jury that are calculated merely to harass or embarrass the juror or to influence his actions in future jury service.

(E) A lawyer shall not conduct or cause, by financial support or otherwise, another to conduct a vexatious or harassing investigation of either a venireman or a juror.

(F) All restrictions imposed by DR 7-108 upon a lawyer also apply to communications with or investigations of members of a family of a venireman or a juror.

(G) A lawyer shall reveal promptly to the court improper conduct by a venireman or a juror, or by another toward a venireman or a juror or a member of his family, of which the lawyer has knowledge.

20. DR 7-109, Contact with Witnesses:

(A) A lawyer shall not suppress any evidence that he or his client has a legal obligation to reveal or produce.

(B) A lawyer shall not advise or cause a person to secrete himself or to leave the jurisdiction of a tribunal for the purpose of making him unavailable as a witness therein.

(C) A lawyer shall not pay, offer to pay, or acquiesce in the payment of compensation to a witness contingent upon the content of his testimony or the outcome of the case. But a lawyer may advance, guarantee, or acquiesce in the payment of:

(1) Expenses reasonably incurred by a witness in attending or testifying.

(2) Reasonable compensation to a witness for his loss of time in attending or testifying.

(3) A reasonable fee for the professional services of an expert witness.

21. DR 7-110, Contact with Officials:

(A) A lawyer shall not give or lend anything of value to a judge, official, or employee of a tribunal.

(B) In an adversary proceeding, a lawyer shall not communicate or cause another to communicate, as to the merits of the cause with a judge or an official before whom the proceeding is pending, except:

(1) In the course of official proceedings in the cause.

(2) In writing if he promptly delivers a copy of the writing to opposing counsel or to the adverse party if he is not represented by a lawyer.

(3) Orally upon adequate notice to opposing counsel or to the adverse party if he is not represented by a lawyer.

(4) As otherwise authorized by law.

22. Standard 3-1.3, Public Statements:

(a) The prosecutor should not exploit the office by means of personal publicity connected with a case before trial, during trial, or thereafter.

(b) The prosecutor should comply with the chapter on Fair Trial and Free Press in these standards. In some instances, as defined in codes of professional responsibility, failure to do so will constitute unprofessional conduct.

(c) In order to assure a fair trial for the accused, the prosecutor and police should cooperate in achieving compliance with the chapter on Fair Trial and Free Press of these standards and codes of professional responsibility.

23. Standard 4-1.3, Public Statements:

(a) The lawyer representing an accused should avoid personal publicity connected with the case before trial, during trial, and thereafter.

(b) The lawyer should comply with the standards on Fair Trial and Free Press herein. In some instances, as defined in codes of professional responsibility, the lawyer's failure to do so will constitute unprofessional conduct.

24. Standard 8-1.1, Extrajudicial Statements by Attorneys:

(a) A lawyer shall not release or authorize the release of information or opinion for dissemination by any means of public communication if such dissemination would pose a clear and present danger to the fairness of the trial.

(b) Subject to paragraph (a), from the commencement of the investigation of a criminal matter until the completion of trial or disposition without trial, a lawyer may be subject to disciplinary action with respect to extrajudicial statements concerning the following matters:

(i) the prior criminal record (including arrests, indictments, or other charges of crime), the character of reputation of the accused, or any opinion as to the accused's guilt or innocence or as to the merits of the case or the evidence in the case;

(ii) the existence or contents of any confession, admission or statement given by the accused, or the refusal or failure of the accused to make a statement;

(iii) the performance of any examinations or tests, or the accused's refusal or failure to submit to an examination or test;

(iv) the identity, testimony, or credibility of prospective witnesses;

(v) the possibility of a plea of guilty to the offenses charged, or other disposition; and

(vi) information which the lawyer knows or has reason to know would be inadmissible as evidence in a trial.

(c) It shall be appropriate for the lawyer, in the discharge of official or professional obligations, to announce the accused's name, age, residence, occupation, family status, and, if the accused has not been apprehended, any further information necessary to aid in the accused's apprehension or to warn the public of any dangers that may exist; to announce the fact and circumstances of arrest (including time and place of arrest, resistance, pursuit, and use of weapons), the identity of the investigating and arresting officer or agency, and the length of the investigation; to announce the identity of the victim if the release of that information is not otherwise prohibited by law; to announce, at the time of seizure a description of any physical evidence (other than a confession, admission, or statement); to announce the nature, substance, or text of the charge, including a brief description of the offense charged; to quote or refer without comment to public records of the court in the case; to announce the scheduling or result of any stage in the judicial process; to request assistance in obtaining evidence and to announce without further comment that the accused denies the charges.

(d) Nothing in this standard is intended to preclude the formulation or application of more restrictive rules relating to the release of information about juvenile offenders, to preclude the holding of hearings or the lawful issuance of reports by legislative, administrative, or investigative bodies, or to preclude any lawyer from replying to charges of misconduct that are publicly made against him or her.

25. Note Chicago Council of Lawyers v. Bauer, infra note 12.

26. See CBS Inc. V. Young, 522 F2d 234 (6th Cir., 1975), and State ex rel Angel v. Woodall, 185 P2d 501 (Mont., 1976).

27. See Society of Professional Journalists v. Martin, 431 F Supp 1182 (S.C., 1977), aff 556 F2d 706 (4th Cir., 1977).

28. See Tribe, American Constitutional Law (1978) at p. 630.

29. 435 US 829 (1978) at pp. 842–46.

30. Infra note 26.

31. Infra note 12. Both rules apparently stem from the 1941 decision of the highest court in Bridges v. California, 314 US 252 (1941).

32. See Wood v. Georgia, 370 US 384 (1962).

33. Standard 8-2.1 deals with the release of criminal information by law enforcement agencies. Standard 8-3.1 prohibits any judicial order that seeks to prevent the press and media from publishing or broadcasting any information in its possession relating to the criminal case. (Note Nebraska Press Assn v. Stuart, 427 US 539 [1976].) Standards 8-3.2 and 803.6(d) impose tight limits on the authority of the trial judge to seal judicial records and to close pre-trial and trial proceedings. (Standard 8-3.2 was rejected by the U.S. Supreme Court in Gannett Co. v. DePasquale, 99 S Ct 2898 [1979].) Standard 8-4.2 recognizes a limited privilege for press and media representatives to publish or broadcast information subject to such court orders if the information has not been acquired by criminal means such as bribery, theft, or fraud.

34. See NYLJ (May 18, 1987) at p. 1.

35. 764 F2d 590 (9th Cir., 1985).

36. See 6 St. Mary's L J 347 (1974) at p. 351.

37. See ABAJ (Sept. 1, 1987) at 29.

38. Local Criminal Court Rule 7(a) of the U.S. District Courts for the Southern and Eastern Districts of New York and also ABA Disciplinary Rule 7-107.

39. 532 F2d 191 (2d Cir., 1976).

40. Infra note 37 at 29.

41. Dkt. 84 Civ 6642 (2d Cir., 1987).

42. See New York Daily News Magazine (March 12, 1985) at 1 et seq.

43. 769 F2d 72 (2d Cir., 1985).

9

Civil Trials and the Right of Access for Press and Media

The civil trial is also open to the public and the press and media under the right of access guaranteed under the First Amendment. Such English legal authorities as Coke, Hale, and Blackstone favored the presumptive openness of the civil trial.[1] Both the state of New Jersey and the commonwealth of Pennsylvania had constitutional provisions favoring free public access to civil trials.[2] Justice Oliver Wendell Holmes in 1884 had declared public access to civil trials to be of "vast importance" for the proper administration of justice.[3] Professor Wigmore opined that public proceedings provide the means whereby public truthworthiness of the trial procedure is achieved.[4]

As early as 1372, the English Parliament had enacted laws governing the right of access to civil court records (that is, a right to inspect and copy judicial records).[5] English common law allowed both a person who needs the document as evidence to enforce a right of access in court and a person who has a proprietary right in the document.[6] In the United States, the right of access to judicial records for all citizens originated with the concept that all citizens should be able to view the government in operation and to learn how it functions.[7]

The Third U.S. Court of Appeals in 1984 in Publicker Industries, Inc. v. Cohen[8] upheld the right of the public and the press and media at common law and under the First Amendment, to be entitled to the right of access to civil proceedings. Here, during a proxy fight to determine control of a publicly held corporation, the federal district court had ordered closure[9] due to the presence in the civil court of a newspaper reporter. The trial court's decision was based on the anticipated discussion of business information that the corporation asserted to be highly sensitive and confidential.[10] In reversing the trial court, Judge Higginbotham spoke of the traditional common law right of access to civil trials possessed by newspapers.[11] He observed that the U.S. Supreme Court had asserted that the primary aim of the First Amendment is to guarantee the uninhibited communication regarding governmental functions at both civil and criminal trials.[12] The trial court should specify the countervailing interest that must be protected if any closure is to result,[13] and therefore it was proper for the trial court to close the civil courtroom only for that part of the hearing during which sensitive and confidential information might be disclosed.[14] Closure with respect to other parts of the hearing was left unexplained by the trial court, and this failure to explain the order constituted both an abuse of discretion by the trial court and a failure to satisfy the designated procedural requirements.[15] In short, the record must show an overriding interest that a closed hearing is necessary to safeguard higher values and is exclusively tailored to serve that purpose.[16] The trial court's sealing of the transcript of the entire hearing was also an abuse of discretion since portions of the hearing should have been available to the press and media.

In Seattle Times Co. v. Rhinehart[17] the U.S. Supreme Court had occasion to rule that, at least in the federal court system, the pre-trial discovery process with its volumes of newsworthy material was not subject to press and media access. The point of the ruling by the highest Court was simply to make it known that the press and media have no special right to gather news; civil cases, in particular, do not require special press and media access if otherwise the civil trial is open and both the judiciary and the government are functioning well, according to the Court. Most importantly, the press and media has no greater right of access to civil trials than the government itself.[18] The so-called "right to know" laws, like the Freedom of Information Act,[19] do not make a distinction between a press and media right of access for news gathering purposes and the public right.[20] It was in Nixon v. Warner Communications, Inc.[21] that the highest Court in 1978 reaffirmed the common law right of access to documents in court proceedings; but, in practice, the limits to the exercise of that right of access depends upon each particular case. But in United States v. Beckham[22] the Sixth U.S. Court of Appeals made a distinction between the right of access to courtrooms and the right of access to tapes and transcripts admitted into evidence. Customarily, court records have been open only for good cause and frequently closed from public view due their private nature or their sensitive nature.[23] Indeed, there is no constitutional access on the civil court side to depositions and other pre-trial documents.[24] But in Avirgan v. Hull[25] the federal district court in Washington, D.C. ruled in December 1987 that a news organization has the right to be present at the pre-trial deposition of a witness in a civil law suit. The particular witness had objected to the presence of the news organization at his deposition.[26] The plaintiffs were a free-lance television cameraman and his wife, a journalist, the cameraman having been wounded at a news conference earlier inside the Nicaraguan border. The court, in opening the civil courtroom to the news organization, declared that the Federal Rules of Civil Procedure directives make such material as depositions open to news organizations unless there was "a factual showing of good cause" why the courtroom should not be open; and "good cause" may not be merely "stereotyped and conclusory statements . . . (but must demonstrate) annoyance, embarrassment, oppression, or undue burden or expense" would result. The court continued: "Ordinarily a deposition is a public document 'freely open to inspection after it is filed with the clerk' . . . and the presumption inherent in Rule 26(c) is that the discovery should be open.[27]

It has been asserted that the right of the public and the press and media for access to civil trials is not as great as in a criminal trial setting.[28] Civil trials are between private parties in a dispute, and generally only the interests of the respective parties are at stake. But the public and the press and media do have a right to know under the First Amendment, as well as an interest in the outcome of the civil litigation, that might very well adversely affect their interests, such as public property, family relationships, and basic speech rights.

The landmark case of Brown v. Board of Education[29] is a ftting example of a civil trial that resolved the issue of segregation of students in public schools solely on the basis of race pursuant to state law. Wht transpires in the courtroom, according to Justice Douglas, is "public property,"[30] and the public and press and media should not be precluded from access to the civil trial. The fair trial strictures of the Sixth Amendment do not pertain to the civil defendant, although the necessity of a fair trial is still inherent in American justice.

In Kemner v. Monsanto Co.,[31] a civil trial involving toxic injuries to sixty-five plaintiffs exposed to the chemical dioxin, the trial judge, in May 1987, the fourth year of the trial, issued an order barring the press and media from "contacting, photographing, filming or interviewing" jurors, members of plaintiffs' families, and employers of plaintiffs. The rationale for this gag order was the preservation of the integrity of the jury. And in Gage v. Bozarth,[32] the Indiana Court of Appeals in May 1987 ruled that an injured plaintiff can be excluded from the civil courtroom during the liability phase of a personal injury action if the plaintiff's appearance would prejudice the jury and if the plaintiff cannot understand the civil proceedings and otherwise assist his counsel.[33] According to the court,

> The party seeking the exclusion must establish that the plaintiff's appearance or conduct is likely to prevent the jury from performing its duty. . . . It is not enough to show the mere existence of a physical or mental injury. . . . Secondly, the trial court must determine whether the plaintiff can understand the proceedings and assist counsel in any meaningful way. If . . . the plaintiff can understand the proceedings and aid counsel, the plaintiff cannot be excluded regardless of prejudicial impact.

Access to documents filed in civil proceedings has been tested in recent years in a series of cases before the federal appellate courts. The Sixth U.S. Court of Appeals in Brown & Williamson Tobacco Corp. v. Federal Trade Commission[34] reversed the trial court's decision to place under seal administrative records and other documents filed by the Federal Trade Commission even though the court admitted that the trial court normally had supervisory power over its own records and files. Here, plaintiff had not overcome the strong presumption in favor of access that attached to judicial records in civil proceedings; plaintiff had not proved a legitimate interest in protecting what plaintiff delineated as a trade secret. The court viewed that argument for trade secret protection as merely a shield to protect plaintiff's reputation against the claim that its cigarettes had no effective filter system. The Seventh U.S. Court of Appeals in In Re Continental Illinois Securities Litigation[35] ruled that the public was entitled to the defendant corporation's special litigation committee report submitted into evidence as part of a shareholder derivative suit. The public has a right to "monitor the functioning of the courts, thereby insuring quality, honesty, and respect for the legal system." The presumption of public and press and media access to the civil courts applied to pre-trial hearings and to evidence introduced in connection with the hearings.[36] And where the court relies on documents as part of the decision-making process, a strong presumption takes over, so that the documents should be made available to the public and the press and media.

In Wilson v. American Motors Corp.,[37] the Eleventh U.S. Court of Appeals considered whether plaintiff should be permitted access to sealed records from an earlier federal court case involving the same defendant; plaintiff sought to establish offensive collateral estoppel.[38] The court authorized release of pleadings, docket entries, orders, filed depositions or affidavits, and transcripts from the hearings and court proceedings but not trial exhibits.[39] Apparently trial exhibits were deemed work products of attorneys and clients and not available to the public and the press and media. A distinctly contrary view—that the public and the press and media do not have a First Amendment right of access to civil court records until after judgment—is found In Re Reporters Committee for Freedom of the Press.[40] Here, the District of Columbia Court of Appeals opined that the trial court had not violated the First Amendment rights of the public and press and media by delaying until after the trial the right to examine certain documents submitted as part of the trial. The court argued that under the common law, no right of public access attached to prejudgment records in civil suit.[41] A public records privilege did not extend to "accusations contained in papers filed by a party and not yet brought before a judge or magistrate for official action."[42] Prejudgment access to documents did not promote the purposes of open trials, according to the court.

The U.S. Supreme Court in 1984 in Seattle Times Co. v. Rhinehart[43] held that "during the last 40 years in which the pre-trial processes have been enormously expanded, it has never occurred to anyone . . . that a pre-trial deposition or pre-trial interrogatories were other than wholly private to the litigants." Courts are indeed aware that pre-trial pleadings often contain scurrilous charges that may never be substantiated, and publication by the press and media of such pre-trial pleadings could well cause irreparable damage. But civil courts, like criminal courts, are open to the public and the press and media so that in every instance it is up to the trial judge to achieve a balance between the rights of the public and press and media and needs of the parties to the civil litigation. The trial judge must carefully weigh all the relevant factors in the light of the facts and circumstances of a particular case.

The juvenile courtroom is unlike the criminal courtroom where adult criminals have their hearings, for offenders in juvenile proceedings are frequently shielded from the public gaze.[44] The rationale for this distinction that pertains to press and media coverage is the rehabilitation basis or underpinnings of the juvenile court system. Treatment, not punishment or criminality, was the focus, and harsh publicity was antithetical to treatment of juvenile offenders. Since the Sixth Amendment is not generally applied to noncriminal proceedings, the right of the accused to a public trial was not guaranteed.[45] Confidentiality of juvenile records and the informal procedure in the juvenile courtroom militated against access by the press and media. On the other hand, public interest in juvenile cases is growing with the tremendous increase in juvenile crime.[46] Openness in the juvenile courtroom has been advocated, although publication or disclosure of juvenile names and addresses should be prohibited. In 1975 in Cox Broadcasting Corp. v. Cohn,[47] the U.S. Supreme Court upheld the freedom of the press as against the right of privacy of a seventeen-year-old rape victim whose name was discovered by the television reporter from examining indictments that had been made available for public inspection in the courtroom. The Court opined that its unwillingness to impose a sanction on the press and media stemmed from the fact that the information was readily obtained from the public domain, the official court records, and therefore "the State must be presumed to have concluded that the public interest was thereby being served."[48]

In Oklahoma Publishing Co. v. District Court,[49] the name and picture of an eleven year old charged with murder had been obtained when the child appeared at a pre-trial detention hearing. The press had been present with the knowledge and apparent consent of the prosecutor, the defense counsel, and the judge, and no objection was observed to the presence of the press until the newspaper stories using the boy's name and photograph appeared also on television. The juvenile court then entered an order prohibiting the further publication or transmission of that information.[50] The Oklahoma Supreme Court upheld the juvenile court's restraining order, relying on the Oklahoma statute that provided that the juvenile proceeding and its records are closed to the public unless ordered open by the judge.[51] The U.S. Supreme Court overturned that decision, noting that all the parties had consented to the presence of the press and media. Later, in Smith v. Daily Mail Publishing Co.,[52] where newspapers, without court approval, printed the identity of a child involved in juvenile proceedings (a West Virginia statute made it a misdemeanor to publish that information), the highest court struck down the statute as deficient under a less-exacting subsequent punishment standard.[53]

Today most states presumptively exclude the public from juvenile proceedings but permit certain persons to attend if they have sufficient interest in the case or in the work of the court.[54] Access to juvenile court records is generally barred for a variety of reasons that seem to be upheld constitutionally.[55]

NOTES

1. See 2 Coke, Institutes of the Laws of England (6th ed., 1681) at p. 103; Hale, History of the Common Law of England (Gray ed., 1971) at p. 163; and 3 Blackstone, Commentaries at p. 373.
2. See Richmond Newspapers, Inc., v. Virginia, 448 US 555 (1980) at p. 567.
3. See Cowley v. Pulsifer, 137 Mass 392 (1884) at p. 394.
4. See 6 Wigmore, Evidence Sec. 1834 (1976) at p. 435; also see 23 Duq L Rev 1227 (1985).
5. See 46 Edw 3 (1372), reprinted in 2 English Statutes at Large 191 196–97 (1341 to 1411); also note 39 Vand L Rev 1465 (1986).
6. See Browne v. Cunningham, 109 Eng Rep 377 (K. B., 1829).
7. See 39 Vand L Rev 1465 (1986) at p. 1467.
8. 733 F2d 1059 (3d Cir., 1984).
9. See Chapter 4 herein.
10. It would appear that the confidential information concerned a failure of the corporation to receive permission in England to introduce a particular enzyme in their grain alcohol used in its whiskey (scotch).
11. Infra note 8 at pp. 1066–67.
12. Citing the Richmond Newspapers case, infra note 2.
13. Citing In Re Iowa Freedom of Information Council, 724 F2d 658 (8th Cir., 1983) at p. 662.
14. Infra note 8 at p. 1072.
15. Infra note 4 at p. 1232.

16. Infra note 8 at p. 1073, citing United States v. Criden, 648 F2d 814 (3d Cir., 1981).

17. 467 US 20 (1984).

18. See Nixon v. Warner Communications, Inc., 435 US 589 (1978).

19. 5 USC 552 (1982); see Warren Freedman, Hazardous Waste Liability (1987) at sec. 3.11.

20. See Case & Comment (November–December 1987) at 23.

21. Infra note 18.

22. 789 F2d 401 (6th Cir., 1986).

23. Infra note 20 at 25.

24. See Anderson v. Cryovac, Inc., 805 F2d 1 (1st Cir., 1986).

25. F Supp (DC, 1987).

26. See New York Times (December 15, 1987) at A22.

27. See NLJ (December 28, 1987) at 8. Also note the Editorial of the Hartford, CT Courant (December 20, 1987) at B2:

Opening pretrial proceedings

Apparently for the first time, a federal judge had declared that a news organization can observe the pretrial questioning of a witness in a civil legal case. The decision will stir controversy among lawyers, who are accustomed to taking depositions (as such sworn testimony is called) behind closed doors. But if it stands, it will serve the public well.

U.S. District Judge Joyce Green ruled in Washington, D.C., that The Village Voice could have a representative attend the deposition proceedings of Glenn A. Robinette, a former CIA employee. Mr. Robinette is being questioned in connection with a damage suit filed against 29 defendants by two free-lance journalists. Their suit, which doesn't name Mr. Robinette as a defendant, stems from a bomb explosion at a 1984 news conference in Nicaragua.

First Amendment lawyers interviewed by The New York Times noted the potential usefulness of Judge Green's ruling in providing public access to information uncovered during the pretrial phase of civil cases. Such cases usually lack the drama of criminal proceedings, but they often involve matters of considerable public interest.

The U.S. Supreme Court hasn't made it clear how much access news reporters and other public observers have to pretrial proceedings, such as depositions and hearings. The access is important for two reasons: Many lawsuits are settled without trials, and judges often make decisions affecting the outcome of trials on the basis of evidence and arguments presented before the trials begin.

Without knowing what happens before trials, therefore, it's impossible for the public to properly evaluate the work of the justice system. Pretrial secrecy simply hides too many pieces of vital information. The secrecy pleases lawyers, judges and litigants who prefer to do such work without public scrutiny, but pretrial proceedings are the the public's business no less than trials.

With great slowness, the courts are opening the pretrial process to the public. Judge Green's order could accelerate the trend, and that's cause for celebration.

The National Law Journal (December 21, 1987) at 12, editorialized about the failure of the U.S. Supreme Court itself to open its own courtroom doors:

And nowhere is that anachronism more pronounced than in the U.S. Supreme Court.

To put it bluntly, there can be no argument against television coverage of the nation's highest court. At that stage, there are no defendants whose rights arguably might be affected by television coverage, there are no witnesses whose identities arguably might need to be protected and there are no victims whose plight might prove embarrassing. And we would like to assume that the lawyers who appear before the high court are some of the nation's top advocates, whose full attention is on their clients and not on self-promotion.

U.S. Chief Justice William H. Rehnquist has indicated he is not opposed to the concept of televising proceedings in the federal court. So we feel that it would be a fitting conclusion to this year of the bicentennial of the Constitution for Justice Rehnquist to announce that he is ready to take whatever steps are necessary to bring his court into the mainstream by allowing broadcast coverage of his court's proceedings.

28. See 23 Duq L Rev 1227 (1985) at p. 1241.

29. 347 US 483 (1954).

30. See Craig v. Harney 331 US 367 (1947) at p. 374.

31. Dkt. 80L970, Illinois Circuit Court, St. Clair County; reported in NLJ (Feb. 9, 1987) at p. 14.

32. Dkt. 92A03-8607-CV-178, Indiana Court of Appeals, 3d Distr., dated March 17, 1987.

33. See NLJ (April 6, 1987) at p. 14.

34. 710 F2d 1165 (6th Cir., 1983).

35. 732 F2d 1302 (7th Cir., 1984).

36. Id. at p. 1309; also see generally 39 Vand L Rev 1465 (1986) at pp. 1481–83.

37. 759 F2d 1568 (11th Cir., 1985).

38. See Warren Freedman, Res Judicata and Collateral Estoppel (Quorum Books, 1987).

39. See Belo Broadcasting Corp. v. Clark, 654 F2d 423 (5th cir., 1981), which barred access to trial exhibits.

40. 773 F2d 1325 (DC Cir., 1985).

41. Id. at pp. 1333–34.

42. Id. at p. 1335, citing Stanford v. Boston Herald-Traveler Corp., 61 NE2d 5 (Mass., 1945).

43. 104 S Ct 2199 (1984).

44. For an excellent treatment of the subject matter, see 17 Colum J & Soc Probs 287 (1982).

45. See Chapter 3 herein.

46. Infra note 44 at pp. 316–17.

47. 420 US 469 (1975).

48. Id. at p. 495.
49. 430 US 308 (1977).
50. Id. at p. 308.
51. 555 P2d 1286 (Okla., 1976).
52. 443 US 97 (1979).
53. Id. at p. 99.
54. See, e.g., Ga. Code Ann. sec. 24A-1801(c) (1981); Haw. Rev. Stat. sec. 571-41 (Supp. 1981); Idaho Code sec. 16-1608 (1979); Ky. Rev. Stat. Ann. sec. 208A.110 (Bobbs-Merrill Supp. 1980) (effective July 1, 1982); Minn. Stat. Ann. sec. 260.155 (West Supp. 1981); Miss. Code Ann. sec. 43-23-15 (1972); Mo. Ann. Stat. sec. 211.171 (Vernon 1959); Nev. Rev. Stat. sec. 62.193 (1979); N. D. Cent. Code sec. 27-20-24 (Supp. 1981); Okla. Stat. Ann. tit. 10, sec. 1111 (West Supp. 1981–1982); 42 Pa. cons. Stat. Ann. sec. 6336(d) (Purdon Supp. 1981); S. C. Code Ann. sec. 14-21-610 (Law. Co-op. 1976); Vt. Stat. Ann. tit. 33, sec. 651 (Supp. 1981); Wash. Rev. Code Ann. sec. 13.34.110 (Supp. 1981); W. Va. Code sec. 49-5-1(d) (Supp. 1981); Wyo. Stat. sec. 14-6-224 (1977).
55. Infra note 33 at p. 333.

10

Public and Press and Media Access to the Courtroom in England

The Third Royal Commission on the Press in 1977 defined freedom of the press as "that degree of freedom from restraint which is essential to enable proprietors, editors and journalists, to advance the public interest by publishing the facts and opinions without which a democratic electorate cannot make responsible judgments."[1] Yet freedom of the press has never become part of the law of England because England has no written constitution; its laws are made piecemeal by Parliament and by the judges of the courts.

In James v. Commonwealth of Australia,[2] the House of Lords opined that "free speech does not mean free speech: it means speech hedged in by all the laws against defamation, blasphemy, sedition, and so forth. It means freedom governed by law." For example, the law prohibits naming rape or blackmail victims; there are limits on reporting evidence in divorce cases; and there are court rules against revealing old criminal convictions. Therefore, in England free speech is what is left of speech after the law has spoken.

Public access to English courts is almost taken for granted.[3] Article 6 of the European Convention on Human Rights (ratified by England in 1951 and enforceable in 1966) guarantees to every defendant a public hearing whenever legal rights are to be determined. As stated in 1913 in Scott v. Scott,[4] "Publicity is the very soul of justice. It is the keenest spur to exertion and the surest of all guards against improbity. It keeps the judge himself while trying under trial." In 1982 Lords

Scarman and Simon pointed out "another important interest involved in justice done openly":

> That the evidence and argument should be publicly known, so that society may judge for itself the quality of justice administered in its name, and whether the law requires modification. . . . The common law by its recognition of the principle of open justice ensures that the public administration of justice will be subject to public scrutiny. Such scrutiny serves no purpose unless it is accompanied by the rights of free speech, i.e., the right publicly to report, to discuss, to comment, to criticize, to impart and to receive ideas and information on the matters subjected to scrutiny. Justice is done in public so that it may be discussed and criticized in public.[5]

But in Home Office v. Harman,[6] a solicitor was held in contempt of court for showing certain documents, read aloud in open court, to journalists. The English Court of Appeal in Regina v. Waterfield,[7] however, upheld the right of the press to remain in the courtroom while the jury was shown allegedly obscene films:

> The public generally are interested in cases of this kind, and for not unworthy reasons. Concepts of sexual morality are changing. Whenever a jury in this class of case returns a verdict, whether of guilty or not guilty, intelligent readers of newspapers and weekly journals may want to know what kind of film was under consideration. Experience during the past decades has shown that every acquittal tends to lead to greater exposure to public gaze of what previous generations thought seemly only in private, if seemly anywhere. Members of the public have the right to depend on the press for information on which to base their opinions.

In England the press, but not the public at large, may attend cases in the juvenile courts,[8] as well as domestic proceedings in magistrates' courts.[9] The press may also attend adult court while a child gives evidence in relation to a sex offense.[10] English judges are empowered to halt all reporting or until the end of a trial.[11] Family disputes are heard in private when details might damage the children of a disrupted marriage. The press "understands"; there is a privileged "press bench" in every English courtroom.

The Official Secrets Act of 1920[12] is an example of the rule that English courts are to be open unless the Crown requests the court to exclude the public during all or part of the evidence.[13] The Crown must persuade the court that publication of the evidence would be prejudicial to the national safety; however, the sentencing of the accused must be passed in public.

Section 41 of the Criminal Justice Act of 1925 prohibits photographing or sketching of jurors, witnesses, party, or judge in the courtroom, the court building, or its precincts. (Tape recordings are prohibited by the Contempt of Court Act of 1981.) Televising the courts is precluded by section 41 of the Criminal Justice Act.[14]

The English Contempt of Court Act[15] expresses the English conviction that the administration of justice by the judiciary is supreme over freedom of the press, as perhaps illustrated by the Sunday Times case[16] in which the House of Lords ruled that a draft article in the newspaper interfering with the administration of justice constituted contempt of court.[17] Following that decision, an appeal was made to the European Court of Human rights,[18] where the newspaper alleged that the United Kingdom had violated Article 10 of the European Convention of Human Rights.[19] Article 10 provides for extensive freedoms of expression, including the "right to impart information and ideas without interference by public authority."[20] The question before the European Court of Human Rights was "whether the rules of contempt of court as applied in the decision of the House of Lords granting the injunction [were] a ground justifying the restriction under Article 10(2)."[21] The court found that the United Kingdom had violated the convention.[22] It might be noted that under the European Convention of Human Rights, an individual has a right of petition for human rights violations, and in the instant case, such an individual as the newspaper owner brought suit against the United Kingdom to enforce and implement the specific legal right that was mandated by the convention of which the United Kingdom was a signatory along with Belgium, Denmark, France, Ireland, Italy, Luxembourg, the Netherlands, Norway, and Sweden.[23] The first step in the process is generally to bring the action before the European Commission[24] but only after the aggrieved party has exhausted all domestic remedies and has applied within six months after the domestic judiciary has rendered a final decision.[25] The usual second step is to bring the matter before the European Court of Human Rights,[26] as was done here; execution of its decisions is generally supervised by the Committee of Ministers.[27]

NOTES

1. See Final Report, Royal Commission on the Press (London: HMSO, 1977).

2. (1936) A. C. 578.

3. See Attorney General v. Leveller Magazine, Ltd. (1979) A. C. 440 (1913) A. C. 417.

4. (1913) A. C. 417.

5. See Home Office v. Harman, (1982) 1 A11 ER 532 at pp. 546–47.

6. Id.

7. (1975) 2 A11 ER 40.

8. See Children and Young Persons Act of 1933, s. 47(2).

9. See Magistrates' Courts Act of 1980, s. 69(2).

10. Infra note 8, sec. 37(1).

11. See Contempt of Court Act of 1981.

12. Sec. 8(4).

13. The New York Times (December 22, 1987) at A16, reported that the British Government was rebuffed on December 21, 1987 in its effort to obtain a permanent injunction against newspaper coverage of charges that the British espionage establishment was penetrated by Soviet agents, which charges were made in a book, *Spycatcher* that had been barred from publication in England, although "bootleg" copies from other countries had been circulated widely in England. The High Court ruled that the Government's argument that national security was at stake in keeping the charges from the public was rejected:

> The absolute protection of the security service could not be achieved this side of the Iron Curtain. . . . The ability of the press freely to report allegations of scandals in government is one of the bulwarks of our democratic society. . . . If the price that has to be paid is the exposure of the Government of the day to pressure or embarrassment when mischievous or false allegations are made, then . . . that price must be paid. . . .

14. Also see In Re St. Andrews (1977) 3 WLR 286.

15. See Report of the Committee on Contempt of Court, CMD No. 5794 (1974); also generally 35 Internat Law and Politics (1984) at pp. 33 et seq.

16. Attorney General v. Times Newspaper Ltd., (1972) 3 WLR 855, revd (1973) 2 WLR 452 (C. A.), revd 1974 A. C. 273.

17. Infra note 15 at pp. 48 et seq.

18. See Convention for the Protection of Human Rights and Fundamental Freedoms, Nov. 4, 1950, 213 UNTS 221; also see 7 Ga J Intl & Comp L 315 (1977).

19. Id.

20. Id. See Articles 52, 53.

21. See 1979 Y. B. Eur Conv on Human Rights 27 and 29 (Judgment of 26 April 1979).

22. Id. at p. 3.

23. From these original ten signatories were added by 1983 eleven other countries: Austria, Cyprus, West Germany, Greece, Iceland, Liechtenstein, Malta, Portugal, Spain, Switzerland, and Turkey. All have ratified the convention except Liechtenstein.

24. Infra note 14 at p. 37.

25. Article 26.

26. See 7 Ga J Intl & Comp L (1977) at p. 323.

27. Articles 30–32.

Bibliography

Law Reviews:

A.B.A.J. (November 1, 1987) at 17.
26 Ariz L Rev 933 (1984).
38 Ark L Rev 403 (1984).
17 Colum J L & Soc Prob 287 (1982).
85 Colum L Rev 1546 (1985).
19 Conn L Rev 561 (1987).
23 Duq L Rev 293 (1984).
16 Ga L Rev 659 (1982).
11 Hastings Con L J 637 (Summer 1984).
94 Harv L Rev 75 (1980).
84 Mich L Rev 475 (December 1985).
National L J (June 22, 1987), Editorial.
14 NM L Rev 401 (Spring 1984).
59 So Cal L Rev 603 (1986).
29 Suffold U L Rev 129 (1985).
1985 Utah L Rev 739 (1985).
39 Vand L Rev 1465 (1986).

Index to Cases

Allgeyer v. Louisiana, 28
Anderson v. Cryovac, Inc., 112
Arkansas Television Co. v. Tedder, 8, 37
Associated Press v. Bell, 7, 19, 37, 69
Associated Press v. District Court, 7
Attorney General v. Leveller Magazine, 118
Attorney General v. Times Newspapers, Ltd., 21, 117, 118
Avirgan v. Hull, 107
Azbill v. Fisher, 21

Belo Broadcasting Corp. v. Clark, 9, 113
Branzburg v. Nixon, 16, 20, 21, 71, 74
Brian W. v. Superior Court, 34
Brown v. Board of Education, 107
Brown & Williamson Tobacco Co. v. FTC, 108-109
Browne v. Cunningham, 111

Cable News Network, Inc. v. U.S. District Court, 77
CBS, Inc. v. Campbell, 21
CBS, Inc. v. Young, 14, 102
Chambers v. Mississippi, 61
Chandler v. Florida, 21, 44, 45-46, 48, 73, 80
Chase v. Robson, 90
Chicago Council of Lawyers v. Bauer, 90, 93, 102
Cinque v. Boyd, 38
Cohen v. Everett City Council, 8
Colton v. U.S., 83
Commonwealth v. Aladjem, 31
Commonwealth v. Fisher, 33
Commonwealth v. Hayes, 37
Commonwealth v. Klinger, 39
Cox Broadcasting Corp. v. Cohn, 12, 61, 110
Craig v. Harney, 43-44, 113
Crowley v. Pulsifer, 9, 111

Daniel v. Dow Jones & Co., 19
Davis v. Alaska, 61
Des Moines Register & Tribune Co. v. Osmundson, 13
Dorfman v. Meiszner, 75

Estes v. Texas, 7, 44-45, 82-83
E. W. Scripps Co. v. Fulton, 2, 8
Ex Parte Washburn, 43, 50

Gage v. Bozarth, 108
Gannett Co. v. De Pasquale, 14, 23, 26, 27, 31, 36, 103
Globe Newspaper Co. v. Superior Court, 6, 24, 36, 38
Griswold v. Connecticut, 27-28, 49

Hirschkop v. Snead, 99
Hirschkop v. Virginia State Bar Assn., 89
Home Office v. Harman, 116, 118
Houchins v. KQED, Inc., 5, 73

In Re Arkansas Bar Assn., 67
In Re Continental Illinois Securities Litigation, 108-109
In Re Express-News Corp., 15
In Re Gault, 34
In Re Globe Newspaper Co., 5
In Re Hearings Concerning Canon 35, 83
In Re Iowa Freedom of Information Council, 111
In Re Matter of the Application to a Judge by the Providence Journal Company and Its Executive Editor, Charles M. Hauser, in Criminal Contempt, 17
In Re Modification of Code of Judicial Conduct Relating to Broadcasting and Photographing Court Proceedings, 67
In Re Oliver, 20, 89, 90
In Re Petition of the Daily Item, 37
In Re Rachmiel, 99
In Re Reporters Committee for Freedom of the Press, 109
In Re St. Andrews, 118
Irvin v. Dowd, 15, 24

James v. Commonwealth of Australia, 115

Kearns-Tribune Corp. v. Lewis, 21, 26
Kemner v. Monsanto Co., 108
KPNX v. Superior Court, 14

Landmark Communications, Inc. v. Virginia, 61, 77, 92-93
Levine v. U.S. District Court, 94
Lindsay v. Lindsay, 38
Lochner v. New York, 28
Lyles v. State, 43

Markfield v. Association of the Bar of the City of New York, 89
Marlowe v. Commonwealth of Kentucky, 38
Martin v. Merola, 95
Martin v. Struthers, 74
Matter of an Application to Conduct Visual Coverage of People v. Larry Davis, 47
Matter of the Application of the Associated Press v. Bell, 35
Miami Herald Publishing Co. v. Lewis, 8
Mills v. Alabama, 18
Murphy v. Florida, 15

National Broadcasting Co. v. Cooperman, 88
Near v. Minnesota, 13
Nebraska Press Assn. v. Stuart, 13, 24, 87-88
New York Post Corp. v. Leibowitz, 74
New York Times Co. v. U.S., 13
Nixon v. Warner Communications, 6, 9, 106-107, 112

Oklahoma Publishing Co. v. District Court, 34, 110
Organization for a Better Austin v. Keefe, 13

Palm Beach Newspapers, Inc. v. Burk, 70
People v. Hagan, 48

People v. Mundy, 41
Phoenix Newspapers, Inc. v. Jennings, 1
Post-Newsweek Stations, Florida, Inc. v. U.S., 21, 78, 79
Powers v. McGuigan, 95
Press-Enterprise Co. v. Superior Court, 3, 25, 36-37
Publicker Industries, Inc. v. Cohen, 105

Red Lion Broadcasting Co. v. FCC, 76-77
Regina v. Waterfield, 116
Richmond Newspapers, Inc. v. Virginia, 3, 6, 19, 21, 27, 28, 36, 71-72, 111
Rideau v. Louisiana, 7, 15, 25
RLR v. State of Alaska, 34
R. W. Page Corp. v. Lumpkin, 8

San Jose–Mercury News v. Municipal Court, 21
Schiavone Construction Co. v. Merola, 95
Scott v. Scott, 115-116
Seattle Times Co. v. Ishikawa, 17
Seattle Times Co. v. Rhinehart, 106, 109-110
Sheppard v. Maxwell, 14, 15, 24, 87
Smith v. Daily Mail Publishing Co., 61, 111
Society of Professional Journalists v. Martin, 102
Stanford v. Boston Herald-Traveler Corp., 113
State ex rel Angel v. Woodall, 102
State ex rel Daily Mail Publishing Co. v. Smith, 20
State ex rel Herald Mail Co. v. Hamilton, 8, 20
State ex rel New Mexico Press Assn. v. Kaufman, 16
State ex rel Oregonian Publishing Co. v. Deiz, 2
State of North Carolina v. Hageman, 21
State of Utah v. Anderson, 16
State of Utah v. Pierre, 21
State v. Burnett, 38
State v. Coe, 75-76
State v. Manley, 42-43
State v. Santos, 48
State v. Smith, 48
State v. Williams, 8

Tofani v. State of Maryland, 20

United Press Assn. v. Valente, 1, 36
United States ex rel Lloyd v. Smallwood v. La Valle, 61
United States ex rel Lloyd v. Vincent, 61
United States ex rel Lloyd v. Yonick v. Briggs, 38
United States v. Beckham, 107
United States v. Biaggi, 7
United States v. Brooklier, 14
United States v. Carolene Products Co., 28
United States v. Criden, 9, 112
United States v. Esposito and Biaggi, 70-71
United States v. Geise, 61
United States v. Hastings, 14-15, 48
United States v. Kerley, 61, 72
United States v. Kobli, 37-38
United States v. Myers, 9
United States v. Raffoul, 7
United States v. Salerno, 70
United States v. Valenzuela-Bernal, 61

Waldo v. Lakeshore Estates, Inc., 91-92
Waller v. Georgia, 8, 26
Washburn v. State, 43, 50
Westmoreland v. CBS, Inc., 77
Wilson v. American Motors Corp., 109
Wood v. Georgia, 103

Zurcher v. Stamford Daily, 72

Subject Index

Aaron Burr trial, 4
ABA: Canons of Professional Ethics, 88; Code of Professional Responsibility, 80-81, 88, 89, 96; Model Rules of Professional Conduct, 80-81, 88; Standards for Criminal Justice, 80; Standards Relating to Fair Trial and Free Press, 79-80, 82, 88, 92
Access, public right of, generally, 1, 3
Act of Parliament (1372), 6
Artist, sketch, 14
Audiotapes, 6

Bail hearings, generally, 5
Bastardy-filiation proceedings, generally, 2
Blackstone, 11-12
Broadcasting, in court, generally, 41 et seq
Broadcasting, states' rights in, generally, 46
Broadcast journalists v. print media, 18-19

Camera, movie, 41
Camera, video, 41
Camera coverage of trial, generally, 14, 41, 72, 79 et seq
Canons of Judicial Ethics, 42
Canon 35, 44
Canon 3A(7), 44, 48, 80
Children and Young Persons Act of 1933, 118
"Circus" in court, 83
Civil rights litigation, generally, 28, 50, 95
Civil trials, generally, 105 et seq
"Clear and present danger" rule, 90, 93
Closure of courtroom, generally, 31, 35
Closure of hearings, generally, 4, 13-14, 27, 106
Code of Judicial Conduct, 17
Columbia Journal of Law and Social Problems, 34-35
Computerized news services, 19
Confession, telecasting of, 7, 69
Contempt, criminal, 17-18, 75
Contempt of Court Act of 1981, 117
Convention for the Protection of Human Rights and Environmental Freedoms, 118
Criminal contempt, 17-18, 75
Criminal Justice Act of 1925, 117

Depositions, discovery, 70, 107
Discovery depositions, 70, 107
Disseminate information, right to, 69 et seq

Electronic media, generally, 79 et seq
England's press and media access to criminal courtroom, 115 et seq
European Convention on Human Rights, 115, 117
European Court of Human Rights, 117, 119
Exclusionary orders of the court, 1

"Fairness doctrine," 18, 76-77
Fair trial, guarantee of, 23
Federal Bar Council, 93, 94-95
Federal Communications Act of 1934, 76-77
Federal Communications Commission, 18, 76-77
Federal Rules of Criminal Procedure, Rule 23, 91; Rule 26(c), 107; Rule 53, 48
Federal Trade Commission, 108-109
First Amendment, 1, 3, 6, 11, 18, 19, 31, 32, 71, 72, 76, 88, 89, 91, 109
Fourteenth Amendment, 23, 28, 33, 49
Freedom of Information Act, 106

"Gag orders," 14, 88
Gather information, right to, 69 et seq
Guardianship proceedings, generally, 2

Heroin, 7
Howard Beach trial, 47

Illinois Juvenile Court Act, 33
Immunity from search warrants, 72

Journalists and reporters, generally, 16
Judicial records or documents, 6
Jury, charge to, 74; impanelling of, 13; system, origins of, 11
Juvenile court model statute, 35
Juvenile criminal courtrooms, 2, 31-32, 34, 110

"Legal Foundations to the Right to Know," 71

"Mafia crime families," 95
Magistrates Courts Act of 1980, 118
Malcolm X murder, 48
Mob boss, 17
"Moots," 3
Motion papers, generally, 70

Narcotics trial, 7
Naturalization proceedings, generally, 42
News services, computerized, 19
New York Constitution, Art. I, Sec. 8, 36
New York House of Refuge, 33
Ninth Amendment, 27

Official Secrets Act of 1920, 116-117
Opening pre-trial proceedings, generally, 112-113
Open proceedings, 1-3

Penitentiary inmates, thirty-eight, 16-17
"Pentagon Papers," 13
Photographing in court, generally, 41
Prejudicial trial publicity, 1, 24, 87 et seq
Preliminary hearings, 3-4, 15-16
Pre-trial bail hearings, 5

Pre-trial suppression hearings, 7, 19, 26, 69
Print media v. broadcast journalists, 18-19
"Prior restraint" rule, 13, 14, 75
Prison conditions, generally, 5, 73
Privacy, right of, 7, 48-49, 70
Proposed Model Guidelines for Telecasting Trials, 61-66
Proxy fights, 105-106
"Public event," defined, 43
Publicity, prejudicial trial, 1, 24, 87 et seq
Public's right of access to criminal courtroom, 1
Public trial, guarantee of, 23

Rape trials, 2, 6-7, 31-32, 110
Reik's "The Compulsion to Confess," 4
Robbery-murder in court, 7

Search warrants, immunity from, 72
Seventh Amendment, 33
Sexual abuse, 24
Sexual offenses, 37-38
"Shield laws," 20
"Shield privilege," 16
Sixth Amendment, 1, 3, 23, 26, 31, 35-36, 49, 72, 79, 87-88, 108, 110
Sketch artist, 14
"Spycatcher," 118
Star Chamber, 11, 26
States' right on broadcasting, 46
"Sunshine laws," 20
Suppression hearings, 7, 19, 26, 69

Tapes, preservation of, 17
Telecast of criminal confession, 7
Televising trials, generally, 41
Third Royal Commission on the Press, 115
Transcripts of trial or hearing: denial of access to, 4, 74; impounding of, 37; preservation of, 17, 74
Trial lawyers, generally, 79 et seq, 87

U.S. District Court for Eastern and Southern Districts of New York Local Rule 7(a), 93-94, 99-100

Waiver of jury trial, 27
Waiver of right to open trial, 2
Warrants, immunity from search, 72
Washburn murder trial, 43, 50
Wiretap information, 5, 70

About the Author

WARREN FREEDMAN was formerly Liability Counsel and Assistant Secretary for Bristol-Myers Corporation. His numerous books on legal topics include *The Right of Privacy in the Computer Age, Frivolous Lawsuits and Frivolous Defenses, Professional Sports and Antitrust,* and *Freedom of Speech on Private Property,* all published by Quorum books.